Gender

She, who had Here so much essentiall joy
As no chance could distract, much lesse destroy;
. . . she to Heaven is gone,
Who made this world in some proportion
A heaven, and here, became unto us all,
Joy, (as our joyes admit) essentiall.

Gender

R. W. Connell

polity

The right of R. W. Connell to be identified as author of this work has been asserted in accordance with the Copyright, Designs and Patents Act 1988.

First published in 2002 by Polity Press in association with Blackwell Publishing Ltd.

Reprinted 2003 (twice)

Editorial office:
Polity Press
65 Bridge Street
Cambridge CB2 1UR, UK

Marketing and production:
Blackwell Publishing Ltd.
108 Cowley Road
Oxford OX4 1JF, UK

Published in the USA by
Blackwell Publishing Inc.
350 Main Street
Malden, MA 02148, USA

A catalogue record for this book is available from the British Library.

Library of Congress Cataloging-in-Publication Data

Connell, R. W.
    Gender / R. W. Connell.
        p.   cm.
    Includes bibliographical references and index.
    ISBN 0-7456-2715-3 (HB : alk. paper) – ISBN 0-7456-2716-1
(PB : alk. paper)
    1. Sex role – Research.   2. Gender identity – Research.
3. Sexology – Research.   I. Title.
HQ1075 .C658   2002
305.3'07'2 – dc21   2001004496

Typeset in 10 on 12 pt Sabon
by Best-set Typesetter Ltd., Hong Kong
Printed in Great Britain by T. J. International, Padstow, Cornwall

This book is printed on acid-free paper.

For further information on polity, please visit our website: http://www.polity.co.uk

Contents

Preface

This book offers a contemporary perspective on gender studies. It starts from the view that gender is a key dimension of personal life, social relations and culture. In this dimension of our lives we face difficult practical issues about identity, social justice and even survival.

But gender is also a topic on which there is an amazing amount of prejudice, ideology, myth, misinformation and outright falsehood. Research and theory in the human sciences offer the best tools for clearing away the rubbish and understanding the real issues.

The book is intended both for students and for scholars. For people new to the field, I introduce key examples of gender research, describe the main results of research on different topics, and provide a map of debates and ideas. I have particularly tried to introduce very recent research, to put readers in touch with current developments and debates.

For people already in the field, I propose an integrated approach to a wide range of issues, from the body and personality differences to the global economy and world peace. I believe there are links between these areas which absolutely require us to move across conventional discipline boundaries. Accordingly, the book draws on a spectrum of human sciences, from psychology and history to international relations, cultural studies, education and sociology.

Gender is a large theme. To understand it well, one must be prepared to travel – both intellectually and culturally. I argue for taking a global perspective on gender, and have tried to present research and ideas from different regions of the world. I am conscious of limits on what I can present, since I read only a few languages, all of them European, and only English fluently. I hope this book will provide a gateway to international discussions, but it cannot claim more than that.

Readers interested in origins will find them in two books where I first tried to reconcile different approaches to gender: *Gender and Power: Society, the Person and Sexual Politics* (1987) and *Which Way is Up? Essays on Sex, Class and Culture* (1983). This book revises the earlier ideas in the light of more recent work, especially:

- post-structuralist and postmodernist ideas about gender, bodies and sexuality;
- the rise of meta-analysis in the psychology of difference;
- the rapid growth of research on men and masculinity;
- new sophisticated research on gender in organizations;
- above all, the growing debate about gender in relation to imperialism, neo-colonialism, and contemporary globalization.

A short book should not be weighed down with long thank-you lists. Most of my intellectual debts will be obvious in the text and references. I am particularly grateful to John Fisher for research assistance, Christabel Draffin for clerical assistance, Patricia Selkirk for expert advice, Carol Hagemann-White for posing crucial questions, Robert Morrell and Ulla Müller for opening cultural worlds for me, Toni Schofield for demanding relevance and Lin Walker for demanding coherence – and to all these people, and other friends, for providing vital encouragement and support. Kylie Benton-Connell has provided support and inspiration in more ways than I can say. The book is dedicated the memory of her mother, and my partner, Pam Benton. The epigraph is from Pam's favourite poet, Donne: 'The second Anniversary'.

R. W. Connell
University of Sydney

The Question of Gender

Recognizing gender

In the year 2000 the American people, with the aid of a number of lawyers, elected a President. The fortunate candidate was a man, George W. Bush. His unfortunate opponent, Al Gore, was also a man. So was Mr Bush's running-mate, who duly became Vice-President. So was Mr Gore's running-mate, who did not. So were seven of the nine Supreme Court justices who made the key decision about which of them would win. Messages of congratulation flooded in from the leaders of other world powers: from the Prime Minister of Great Britain, a man; the Prime Minister of Japan, a man; the Chancellor of Germany, a man; the Prime Minister of France, a man; the President of the Russian Federation, a man; the President of the People's Republic of China, a man. They are not exceptional. On the most recent count, 93 per cent of all cabinet ministers in the world's governments are men.

The year before, the American people were troubled by extraordinary violence in the country's schools. The Columbine high school massacre was the peak in a pattern of killings where one or two pupils take guns to the school they attend and shoot fellow pupils and teachers. Some of the dead were girls, but none of the killers were. It seems that an established pattern of violence among men has now appeared among teenage boys as well.

Multiple killings are not unique to the United States. In January 1996 there was a multiple murder in the state of Queensland in Australia.

Three children had been found shot to death in a car parked outside a house in which four adults were found dead. A wife, fearing her violent husband, had left him and was living in hiding with her parents. Apparently the husband extracted her address from the children while they were on a custody visit, then murdered them, murdered her, murdered her parents, and finally shot himself. This was one of twenty-eight multiple killings with guns in Australia from 1987 to 1996. All twenty-eight killers were men. Men are much more likely than women to own weapons – by a ratio of four to one, according to research on gun ownership in the USA.

Women do most of the housework, in most contemporary societies, and also most of the work of caring for young children. Women are much less likely to be present in the public realm than men, and when they are, usually have less in the way of resources. For instance, in almost all parts of the world men are more likely than women to have a paid job. The world 'economic activity rate' for women is just over two-thirds of the rate for men, according to 1997 figures. The main exceptions are former Soviet countries and parts of west Africa, where women's economic participation rates are unusually high. But in Arab states women's participation rates are as low as one-fifth the rate for men, and in south Asia and Latin America they are about half the rate for men.

When women do get jobs, their average wages are lower than men's. And partly for this reason, women's average incomes are much lower than men's, though women do at least as many hours of work as men, and often more. It is a notable fact – in the light of claims that we live in a 'post-feminist' world where equality has been achieved – that women's average incomes, world-wide, are 56 per cent of men's average incomes. Accordingly, most women in the world, especially women with children, are economically dependent on men. And in many parts of the world some men believe that women who are dependent on them must be their property – to discard if they wish, to kill if need be.

Four decades after the Women's Liberation movement criticized sexist stereotypes, Western media are still packed with images of female passivity. On my way to work I pass a newsagency which displays the posters for the week's mass-circulation magazines. Almost every poster shows a young woman: usually blonde, always dangerously thin, heavily made up, pretty, and not doing anything. Girls are still taught by mass culture that they need above all to be desirable, as if their main task were to lie on silk cushions waiting for Prince Charming to come, checking the horoscope from week to week to learn if their star signs will be compatible when he arrives.

Boys are not generally taught to make themselves attractive. Rather they are taught the importance of appearing hard and dominant – whether they feel like it or not. At school and in the media boys are steered towards competitive sports, and are often put under heavy peer pressure to show their toughness. Not surprisingly, it is mainly young men who are recruited into jobs that require the use of force: police, the military, private security, and blue-collar crime. And it is mainly young women who are recruited into jobs that repair the consequences of violence: nursing, psychology, and social work.

Here we have diverse facts – about politics, about violence, about economics, about mass culture, about childhood and youth. Recognizing that they are all connected is the basis of modern thought about gender. These facts form a pattern, which we may call the gender arrangements or 'gender order' of contemporary society.

Recognizing the gender order is easy; understanding it is not. Creative thinkers such as Simone de Beauvoir and Juliet Mitchell, and social movements such as Women's Liberation, have pointed out the gender patterns and tried to change them. But their ideas have always been contested. A number of conflicting theories of gender now exist, and some issues about gender are still very difficult to resolve. At the same time, there is now a large volume of research on gender questions, some of it very good; and there is a growing fund of practical experience with gender reform.

Understanding gender

In everyday life we normally take gender for granted. We instantly recognize a person as a man or woman, girl or boy. We arrange much of our everyday business around the distinction. Conventional marriages require one of each. Mixed doubles tennis requires two of each, but most sports require one kind at a time. The most popular television broadcast in the world is said to be the American Super Bowl, in which a hundred million people watch a strikingly gendered event: large armoured men crash into each other in pursuit of a leather ball, and thin women in short skirts dance and smile in the pauses. Most of us cannot crash or dance so well, but we do our best in other ways. As men or women we slip our feet into differently shaped shoes, button our shirts on opposite sides, get our heads clipped by different hairdressers, buy our pants in separate shops, and take them off in separate toilets.

These arrangements are so common, so familiar, that they can seem part of the order of nature. Belief that gender distinction is 'natural' makes it scandalous when people don't follow the pattern – for instance, when people of the same gender fall in love with each other. So homosexuality is declared 'unnatural' and bad. The same issue of the Australian newspaper that reported the multiple killing in 1996 also reported a new move by the government of the state of Tasmania. As part of its law-and-order package in the run-up to a state election, the penalty for men having sex with other men in their own homes was to be raised from twenty-one to twenty-five years in jail.

But if having sex with another man is unnatural, why have a law against it? We don't provide penalties for violating the third law of thermodynamics. The proposed Tasmanian law – like anti-gay ordinances in United States cities, like the criminalization of women's adultery in Islamic Sharia law – only makes sense because the matter is not fixed by nature. These laws are part of an enormous social effort to channel people's behaviour. Ideas about gender-appropriate behaviour are constantly being circulated, not only by legislators but also by priests, parents, teachers, advertisers, retail mall owners, talk-show hosts and disk jockeys. Events like the Super Bowl are not just consequences of our ideas about gender difference. They also help to create and disseminate gender difference, by displays of exemplary masculinities and femininities.

Being a man or a woman, then, is not a fixed state. It is a becoming, a condition actively under construction. The pioneering French feminist Simone de Beauvoir put this in a classic phrase: 'One is not born, but rather becomes, a woman'. Though the positions of women and men are not simply parallel, the principle is also true for men: one is not born masculine, but acquires and enacts masculinity, and so becomes a man. As de Beauvoir further saw – following the pioneering psychoanalyst Sigmund Freud – this 'becoming' follows many different paths, involves many tensions and ambiguities, and may produce unstable results. Part of the mystery of gender is how a pattern that on the surface appears so stark and rigid, on close examination turns out so fluid, complex and uncertain.

So we cannot think of womanhood or manhood as fixed by nature. But neither should we think of them as simply imposed from outside, by social norms or pressure from authorities. People construct themselves as masculine or feminine. We claim a place in the gender order – or respond to the place we have been given – by the way we conduct ourselves in everyday life.

Most people do this willingly, and often enjoy the gender polarity. Wearing leather jacket and engineer boots, my body declares: I am pleased to be masculine; I cultivate toughness, hard edges, assertiveness. Wearing lace collar and ruffled skirt, my body declares: I am pleased to be feminine; I cultivate softness, smooth and rounded forms, receptiveness. In Western culture, sexual pleasure is often organized around gender polarity. Most of us desire either men or women, but not both. What is gender-ambiguous is often an object of disgust or derision: 'You can't tell them apart nowadays . . .'

Yet gender ambiguities are not so rare. There are masculine women and feminine men. There are women in love with other women, and men in love with other men. There are people who enjoy both leather jackets and ruffled skirts. There are women who are heads of households, and men who bring up children. There are women who are soldiers and men who are nurses.

Psychological research suggests that the great majority of us combine masculine and feminine characteristics, in varying blends, rather than being all one or all the other. Gender ambiguity can be an object of fascination and desire, as well as disgust. Gender impersonations are familiar in both popular and high culture, from the cross-dressed actors of Shakespeare's stage to drag movies like *Tootsie* and *Priscilla*.

There is certainly enough gender blending to provoke heated reminders from fundamentalist preachers, conservative politicians and football coaches – categories which increasingly overlap – that we ought to be what we naturally are, dichotomous. There are whole social movements dedicated to re-establishing 'the traditional family', 'true femininity' or 'real masculinity'. These movements are themselves clear evidence that the boundaries they defend are none too stable.

But the effort to sustain the gender categories also sustains the relations between them – and therefore sustains the inequalities they produce, and the harm they do. The inequalities of income and political authority already mentioned are part of a larger pattern of inequalities between women and men. Most wealth is in the hands of men, most big institutions are run by men, most science and technology is controlled by men. In many countries, including big populations such as Bangladesh, India, Nigeria and Egypt, women are much less likely than men to have even been taught to read. On a world scale, two-thirds of illiterate people are women. In countries like the United States, Australia and Germany middle-class women have gained full access to higher education and have made inroads into middle management and professions. But as the US Congress's Glass Ceiling Commission recently showed, even in those countries many informal barriers operate to keep the top levels of power and wealth still a world of men. Of the senior managers of major US corporations 95 to 97 per cent are men.

There is also unequal respect. In many situations, including the cheerleaders at the football game, women are treated as marginal to the main action, or as just the objects of men's desire. Whole genres of humour – bimbo jokes, woman-driver jokes, wife jokes, mother-in-law jokes, spinster jokes, dumb-whore jokes, rolling-pin jokes – are based on contempt for women's triviality and stupidity. A whole industry, ranging from heavy pornography and prostitution to soft-core advertising, markets women's bodies as objects of consumption by men. Equal-opportunity reforms in the workplace often run into a refusal by men to be under the authority of a woman. The same happens in many religions, among them Catholic Christianity, mainstream Islam, and some sects of Buddhism. All of these prevent women from holding major religious office, and often treat women symbolically as a source of defilement for men.

Though men in general benefit from the inequalities of the gender order, they do not benefit equally. Indeed, many pay a considerable price. Boys and men who depart from dominant definitions of masculinity because they are gay, effeminate, or simply wimpish, are often subject to verbal abuse and discrimination, and are sometimes the targets of violence. Men who conform to dominant definitions of masculinity may also pay a price. As research on men's health shows, men have a higher rate of industrial accidents than women, have a higher rate of death by violence, more alcohol abuse, and (not surprisingly) more sporting injuries. Men of marginalized ethnic groups may be targeted for racist abuse and are likely to have the poorest working conditions, health status and life expectancy.

Gender arrangements are thus, at the same time, sources of pleasure, recognition and identity, and sources of injustice and harm. This means that gender is inherently political – but it also means the politics can be complicated and difficult.

Inequality and oppression in the gender order have repeatedly led to demands for reform. Movements for change include the nineteenth-century campaigns for married women's property rights and votes for women, and twentieth-century campaigns for homosexual law reform, women's trade unionism, equal employment opportunity, women's reproductive rights, and the prevention of rape and domestic violence.

Political campaigns resisting some of these changes, or seeking counter-changes, have also arisen. The scene of gender politics currently includes anti-gay campaigns, anti-abortion ('pro-life') campaigns, a spectrum of men's movements, and a complex international debate about links between Western feminism and Western cultural dominance in the world.

In this history, the Women's Liberation and Gay Liberation movements of the 1960s–1970s were pivotal. They did not reach all their political goals, but they had a profound cultural impact. They called attention to a whole realm of human reality that was poorly understood, and thus created a demand for understanding as well as action. This is the historical take-off point of contemporary gender research. Political practice launched a deep change – which increasingly seems like a revolution – in human knowledge.

This book is an attempt to map this revolution. It will describe the terrain revealed by gender politics and gender research, introduce the debates about how to understand it and change it, and offer solutions to some of the problems these debates have run into. In chapter 2 I discuss four notable examples of recent gender research, to show how the broad issues just discussed take shape in specific investigations. Chapter 3 turns to the issue of 'difference', the extent of sex differences, and the way bodies and society interact. This requires an account of gender as a social structure, which I present in chapter 4, exploring the different dimensions of gender and the process of historical change. Chapters 5 and 6 discuss gender on the small scale, in personal life, and the rather different issues raised by gender on the large scale, in institutions and world society. Chapters 7 and 8 address gender theory and gender politics, mapping the growth of understanding, the conflicts of ideas, and what is at stake in movements for change. This raises questions both about the micro-politics of personal life, and the large-scale politics of institutions and movements, ending with a discussion of gender politics in world society.

Defining gender

As a new awareness of issues developed, a new terminology was needed. Over the last thirty years the term 'gender' has become common in English-language discussions to describe the whole field (though it has never been universally accepted). The term was borrowed from grammar. Ultimately it comes from an ancient Indo-European word-root meaning 'to produce' (cf. 'generate'), which gave rise to words in many languages meaning 'kind' or 'class' (e.g. 'genus'). In grammar 'gender' came to refer to the specific distinction between classes of nouns 'corresponding more or less' – as the nineteenth-century *Oxford English Dictionary* primly noted – 'to distinctions of sex (and absence of sex) in the objects denoted'. Grammar suggests how widely such distinctions permeate human cultures. In many languages not only the words for people are gendered, but also the words for objects, concepts and states of mind.

Language is an important aspect of gender, but does not provide a consistent framework for understanding it. Languages engender concepts in different ways. For instance 'terror' is feminine in French ('la terreur'), masculine in German ('der Schrecken'), and neuter in English. Different languages make different distinctions. English is a relatively un-gendered language (among its few gender distinctions are the pronouns 'he', 'she' and 'it'). Yet English has both 'sex' and 'gender' where German has one word, 'Geschlecht'. Japanese does not have a closely analogous word at all – so a Japanese text on gender transliterates the English word.

Many languages define a trichotomy of classes: masculine, feminine and neuter. Most contemporary discussions of gender in society, however, drop the third category and emphasize a dichotomy. Starting from a presumed biological divide between male and female, they define gender as the social or psychological difference that corresponds to that divide, elaborates it, or is caused by it.

In its most common usage, then, the term 'gender' means the cultural difference of women from men, based on the biological division between male and female. Dichotomy and difference are the substance of the idea. Men are from Mars, women are from Venus.

There are decisive objections to such a definition:

- Human life does not simply divide into two realms, nor does human character divide into two types. Our images of gender are often dichotomous, but the reality is not. Abundant evidence will be seen throughout this book.
- A definition in terms of difference means that where we cannot see difference, we cannot see gender. With such a definition we could not recognize the gendered character of lesbian or homosexual desire (based on gender similarity), nor the powerful gender dynamic of an all-male army. We would be thrown into confusion by research which found only small psychological differences between women and men, which would seem to imply that gender had evaporated. (See chapter 3.)

- A definition based on dichotomy excludes the patterns of difference *among* women, and among men, from the concept of gender. But there are such differences that are highly relevant to the pattern of relations between women and men. For instance, the difference between violent and non-violent masculinities matters a lot, and so does the difference between femininities which are oriented to heterosexual relations and those which are not. (See chapter 5.)
- A definition in terms of personal characteristics ignores processes which lie beyond the individual person. Large-scale social processes are based on the *shared* capacities of women and men more than on their differences. The creation of goods and services in a modern economy is a major example: it is the common capacities of women and men as workers that matters most to the productivity of industry. Yet the products of the process – the wealth generated, for instance – may be distributed in highly gendered ways.

The development of social science has provided a way past these difficulties. The key is to move from a focus on difference to a focus on *relations*. Gender is, above all, a matter of the social relations within which individuals and groups act.

Gender relations do include difference and dichotomy, but also include many other patterns. For instance, gender in the contemporary world involves massive hierarchies of power among men – as seen in multinational corporations, or armies – which can in no sense be reduced to 'male/female differences', however caused.

Enduring or extensive patterns among social relations are what social theory calls 'structures'. In this sense, gender must be understood as a social structure. It is not an expression of biology, nor a fixed dichotomy in human life or character. It is a pattern in our social arrangements, and in the everyday activities or practices which those arrangements govern.

Gender is a social structure, but of a particular kind. Gender involves a specific relationship with bodies. This is recognized in the commonsense definition of gender as an expression of natural difference, the bodily difference of male from female. What is wrong with this formula is not the attention to bodies, nor the concern with sexual reproduction, but the idea that cultural patterns simply 'express' bodily difference.

Sometimes cultural patterns do express bodily difference. But often they do more than that, or less than that, or something else completely.

In relation to the distinction of male from female bodies, social practices sometimes exaggerate (e.g. maternity clothes), sometimes deny (many employment practices), sometimes mythologize (computer games), sometimes complicate ('third gender' customs). So we cannot say that social arrangements routinely 'express' biological difference.

But we can say that, in a variety of ways, society *addresses* bodies and puts reproductive difference into play. There is no fixed 'biological base' for the social process of gender. Rather, there is an arena in which bodies are brought into social processes, in which our social conduct does something with reproductive difference. I will call this the 'reproductive arena'.

This allows a definition of gender that escapes the paradoxes of 'difference'. *Gender is the structure of social relations that centres on the reproductive arena, and the set of practices (governed by this structure) that bring reproductive distinctions between bodies into social processes.* To put it informally, gender concerns the way human society deals with human bodies, and the many consequences of that 'dealing' in our personal lives and our collective fate. The terms used in this definition are explained more fully in chapters 3 and 4 below.

This definition has important consequences. Among them: Gender patterns may differ strikingly from one cultural context to another, but are still 'gender'. Gender arrangements are reproduced socially (not biologically) by the power of structures to constrain individual action, so they often appear unchanging. Yet gender arrangements are in fact always changing, as human practice creates new situations and as structures develop crisis tendencies. Finally, gender may have an end. Each of these points will be explored later in the book.

Note on sources

Most of the statistics mentioned in this chapter, such as income, economic activity rates and literacy, can be found in United Nations Development Programme (1999; see list of references at back of book). Figures on parliamentary representation and numbers of ministers are from Inter-Parliamentary Union (1999), and on managers, from Glass Ceiling Commission (1995b). Sources of information on men's health can be found in Schofield et al. (2000). A report on the murder-suicide case referred to is in the *Sydney Morning Herald*, 26 Jan. 1996, p. 1, and on the Tasmanian government anti-gay initiative, p. 3. For gun massacres in Australia see Crook and Harding (1997), and for gun ownership in the USA see Smith and Smith (1994). The quotation on 'woman' is from de Beauvoir's *The Second Sex* (1949: 295). Definitions and etymology of the word 'gender' are in *The Oxford English Dictionary*, vol. 4, Oxford, Clarendon Press, 1933, p. 100.

2

Schools, Mines, Sex and War

Often research is best approached through specific examples. In this chapter I will discuss four of the most notable examples of gender analysis published in the last decade. Three of them focus on everyday life in particular settings – a school, a workplace, a personal life – and one deals with gender change in a great historical transition. These studies come from four continents and deal with very different issues. Yet it is possible to see in them some of the common themes of gender research.

Case 1: The play of gender in school life

Everyone knows what a school is. One of the most difficult tasks in social research is to take a situation that everyone thinks they understand, and illuminate it in new ways. This is what the American ethnographer Barrie Thorne achieves in her subtly observed and highly readable book *Gender Play* (1993).

At the time Thorne started her work, children were not much discussed in gender research. When they were mentioned, it was usually assumed that they were being 'socialized' into gender roles, in a top-down transmission from the adult world. It was generally assumed that there are two sex roles, a male one and a female one, with boys and girls getting separately inducted into the norms and expectations of the appropriate one. This idea was based on a certain amount of research using paper-and-pencil questionnaires, but not on much actual observation of gender in children's lives.

Thorne did that observation. Her book is based on fieldwork in two North American elementary (primary) schools. She spent eight months in one, three months in another, hanging about in classrooms, hallways and playgrounds, talking to everyone and watching the way the children interacted with each other and with their teachers in work and play.

Ethnography as a method sounds easy, but in practice is hard to do well. Part of the problem is the mass of information an observer can get from just a single day 'in the field'. You need to know what you are looking for. But you also need to be open to new experiences and new information, able to see things that you did not expect to see.

As an observer Thorne was certainly interested in transmission from older people, in the ways children pick up the details of how to do gender. Her funniest (and perhaps also saddest) chapter is called 'Lip Gloss and "Goin' With" ', about how pre-adolescent children learn the techniques of teenage flirting and dating. She was also interested in the differences between the girls' and the boys' informal interactions – the different games they played, spaces they used, words they spoke, and so on.

But Thorne was able to see beyond the patterns described in conventional gender models. She became aware how much these models predisposed an observer to look for difference. She began to pay attention, not only to the moments in school life when the boys and girls separated, but also to the moments when they came together. She began to think of gender difference as *situational*, as created in some situations and ignored or overridden in others. Even in recess-time games, where the girls and boys were usually clustered in separate parts of the playground, they sometimes moved into mixed activities without any emphasis on difference. There were many 'relaxed cross-sex interactions' in the school's daily routine. Clearly, the boys and girls were not permanently in separate spheres, nor permanently enacting opposite 'sex roles'.

Recognizing this opened up a number of other issues. What were the situations where gender was emphasized or de-emphasized? Thorne noticed that, though teachers sometimes emphasized gender – for instance, setting up a classroom learning game with the girls competing against the boys – most teacher-controlled activities de-emphasized gender. This is true, for instance, of the commonest teaching technique in schools, the 'talk-and-chalk' method where the teacher at the front of the room demands the attention of all the pupils to an exposition of some lesson that they all have to learn. In this situation the basic division is between teacher and taught, not between groups of pupils; so girls and boys are in the same boat.

Next, how did the children establish gender difference when they did emphasize it? Thorne began to identify a kind of activity she called 'borderwork': 'When gender boundaries are activated, the loose aggregations "boys and girls" consolidates into "the boys" and "the girls" as separate and reified groups. In the process, categories of identity that on other occasions have minimal relevance for interaction become the basis of separate collectivities' (1993: 65).

There are different kinds of borderwork in a primary school. One of the most interesting is chasing, a kind of game that is sometimes very fluid and sometimes not. I remember a chasing game at my primary school, a rather intimidating game called 'cocky-laura', which was extremely rule-bound. One of the implicit rules was that only boys could play, because the girls were forbidden by the school to be in the part of the playground where a big gum-tree stood that was one of the bases. In the schools Thorne studied, boys and girls could play together, and often chased each other, playing 'girls-chase-the-boys' and 'boys-chase-the-girls'. Indeed the one game would often merge into the other, as the chased turned around and became the chasers. Thorne notes that often boys chased boys, or girls chased girls, but these patterns attracted little attention or discussion. However girls-chasing-boys/boys-chasing-girls often resulted in lively discussion and excitement. It was a situation in which

> Gender terms blatantly override individual identities, especially in references to the other team ('Help, a girl's chasin' me'; 'C'mon Sarah, let's get that boy'; 'Tony, help save me from the girls'). Individuals may call for help from, or offer help to, others of their gender. And in acts of treason, they may grab someone from their team and turn them over to the other side. For example, in an elaborate chasing scene among a group of Ashton third-graders, Ryan grabbed Billy from behind, wrestling him to the ground. 'Hey girls, get 'im,' Ryan called. (1993: 69)

Thorne's observation of children might alert us to parallel processes among adults. Borderwork is constantly being done to mark gender boundaries, if not by chasing then by jokes, dress, forms of speech, etc. Gender difference is not something that simply exists; it is something that happens, and must be made to happen; something, also, that can be un-made, altered, made less important.

The games in which the children make gender happen do something more. When the girls chase the boys and the boys chase the girls, they seem to be acting equally, and in some respects they are – but not in all respects. For a rough-and-tumble version of the chasing game is more common among the boys. Boys normally control more of the playground space than the girls do, more often invade girls' groups and disrupt the girls' activities than the girls disrupt theirs. That is to say, the boys more often make an aggressive move and a claim to power, in the limited sense that children can do this.

In the symbolic realm, too, the boys claim power. They treat girls as a source of contamination or pollution, for instance calling low-status boys 'girls' or pushing them next to the space occupied by girls. The girls do not treat the boys that way. Girls are more often defined as giving the imaginary disease called 'cooties', and low-status girls may get called 'cootie queens'. A version of cooties played in one of the schools is called 'girl stain'. All these may seem small matters. But as Thorne remarks, 'recoiling from physical proximity with another person and their belongings because they are perceived as contaminating is a powerful statement of social distance and claimed superiority' (1993: 75).

So there is an asymmetry in the situations of boys and girls, which is reflected in differences among the boys and among the girls. Some boys often interrupt the girls' games, other boys do not. Some boys have higher status, others have lower. Some of the girls move earlier than others into 'romance'. By fourth grade, homophobic insults – such as calling another boy a 'fag' – are becoming common among the boys, most of whom learn that this word is a way of expressing hostility before they know what its sexual meaning is. At the same time, however, physical contact among the boys is becoming less common – they are learning to fear, or be suspicious of, displays of affection. In short, the children are beginning to show something of the differentiation of gender patterns, and the gender and sexual hierarchies, that are familiar among adults.

There is much more in Thorne's fascinating book, including a humorous and insightful discussion of what it is like for an adult to do research among children. For me, the most important lesson her book teaches is about these American children's *agency* in learning gender. They are not passively 'socialized' into a sex role. They are, of course, learning things from the adult world around them: lessons about available identities, lessons about performance, and – regrettably – lessons about hatred. But they do this actively, and on their own terms. They find gender interesting and sometimes exciting. They move into and out of gender-based groupings. They sometimes shore up, and sometimes move across, gender boundaries. They even play with and against the gender dichotomy itself. Gender is important in their world, but it is important as a human issue that they deal with, not as a fixed framework that reduces them to puppets.

Case 2: Manhood and the mines

In the late nineteenth century the fabulous wealth of the largest gold deposit in the world began to be exploited by the Dutch and British settler communities in South Africa. The Witwatersrand (Whitewater Ridge) gold deposits were immense. But the ore was low-grade, so huge volumes had to be processed. And the main deposits lay far below the high plateau of the Transvaal, so the mines had to go deep. The first wild gold rushes soon turned into an organized industry dominated by large companies, with a total workforce of hundreds of thousands.

Because the price of gold on the world market was fixed, the companies' profitability depended on keeping labour costs down. Thus the industry needed a large but low-paid workforce for demanding and dangerous conditions underground. To colonial entrepreneurs, the answer was obvious: indigenous men. So black African men, recruited from many parts of South Africa and even beyond, became the main labour force of the gold industry – and have remained so ever since.

Over a twenty-year period T. Dunbar Moodie worked with a series of partners to document the experience of men who made up this labour force, a key group in South Africa's history. Their story is told in his book *Going for Gold* (1994). Moodie studied the company archives and government records, directed participant-observation studies, interviewed miners, mine executives and women in the 'townships' where black workers lived. A key moment came when one of his collaborators, Vivienne Ndatshe, interviewed forty *retired* miners in their home country, Pondoland (near the south-eastern coast). Her interviews revealed aspects of the miners' experience which changed the picture of migrant labour profoundly.

Because the mines were large-scale industrial enterprises owned by European capital, it had been easy to think of the mineworkers as 'proletarians' on the model of European urban industrial workers. But the reality was different. The racial structure of the South African workforce – whites as managers, blacks providing the labour – might have kept labour costs down, but also created a barrier behind which the mineworkers could sustain cultures of their own, and exercise some informal control over their work. Most lived in all-male compounds near the mines, where they had to create their own social lives.

When the men signed on with recruiting agents – generally on con-
tracts lasting four months to two years – and set off on the journey of
hundreds of kilometres to the mines, they did not take families with them
and did not intend to become city dwellers. This was not just because
the wages were too low to support families in the cash economy of the
cities. More importantly, the mineworkers mostly came from areas with
a smallholder agricultural economy, such as Pondoland. They kept their
links to that economy, and intended to return to it.

For most of them the point of earning wages at the mine was to sub-
sidize rural households run by their families, or to accumulate resources
that would allow them to establish new rural households on their return
– buying cattle, financing marriages, etc. Being the wise and respected
head of a self-sufficient homestead was the ideal of 'manhood' to which
Mpondo migrant workers (alongside others) subscribed. The mine work
was a means to this end.

This situation led to gender practices very different from those of the
conventional European breadwinner/housewife couple. First, the men
working at the mines and living in the compounds had to provide their
own domestic labour, and if sexually active, find new sexual partners.
Some went to women working in nearby towns. Others created sexual
and domestic partnerships, known as 'mine marriages', between older
and younger men in the compounds. In such an arrangement the young
man did housework and provided sexual services in exchange for gifts,
guidance, protection and money from the senior man. This was a well-
established if discreet custom, which lasted for decades. For the individual partners it was likely to be temporary. In due course the younger man
would move on; he might in turn acquire a 'mine wife' if he became a
senior man in a compound. These relationships were not taken back to
the homeland.

Back in the homeland, the rural homesteads had to keep functioning
while many of their men were away at the mines. This too led to a significant adjustment, because the person left to run the homestead might
well be a woman, such as the mineworker's wife. Now the older Mpondo
men did not define manhood, *ubudoda*, in terms of warrior virtues, but
in a very different way. As one ex-miner, Msana, put it:

'Ubudoda is to help people. If somebody's children don't have books
or school fees or so, then you are going to help those children while
the father cannot manage. Or if there is somebody who died, you go
there and talk to people there. Or, if someone is poor – has no oxen
– then you can take your own oxen and plow his fields. That is

ubudoda, one who helps other people.' [Moodie writes:] I . . . asked whether there was not also a sort of manhood displayed by strength in fighting. Msana replied at once: 'No, that is not manhood. Such a person is called a killer.' (1994: 38)

Manhood, in this cultural setting, principally meant competent and benevolent management of a rural homestead, and participation in its community. Since a woman could perform these tasks, almost all the older Mpondo men logically held the view that a woman could have *ubudoda*. They were not denying that in a patriarchal society men ultimately have control. But they emphasized a conception of partnership between women and men in the building of homesteads, in which women could and often did perform masculine functions and thus participated in manhood.

But these gender arrangements, brought into existence by specific historical circumstances, were open to change. As the twentieth century wore on, the homestead agricultural economy declined. The apartheid government's policies of resettlement disrupted communities and created huge pools of displaced labour. The gold mining industry also changed. The workers became increasingly unionized, the mine managements abandoned old forms of paternalism and sought new ways of negotiating with workers (though they continued to foment 'tribal' jealousies). In the 1970s the old wage rates were abandoned and miners' incomes began to climb. This made it possible to support an urban household, or a non-agricultural household in the countryside, and broke the economic symbiosis between homestead and mine.

In these changed circumstances the old migrant cultures were eroded, including their distinctive gender patterns. Younger Mpondo men no longer define 'manhood' in terms of presiding over a rural homestead. They simply equate it with the biological fact of maleness – which women cannot share. 'Thus,' remarks Moodie, 'for the present generation of Mpondo, maleness and femaleness have been dichotomized again.' The women with manhood have disappeared from the scene.

Proletarianization has arrived at last, and with it a gender ideology closer to the European pattern. Among the younger mineworkers – more unionized, more militant and much better paid than their fathers – masculinity is increasingly associated with toughness, physical dominance, and aggressiveness. This pattern of masculinity requires no reciprocity with women, who are, increasingly, left in the position of housewives dependent on a male wage earner.

There is much more in Moodie's complex and gripping work than can be summarized here: the labour process in the mines, life in the compounds, episodes of violence and resistance. As with Thorne's *Gender Play*, I am struck by the evidence of people's active creation of gender patterns. But the story of the mines gives a stronger impression of the constraints under which this creation is done, the impact of economic and political forces. There is a clearer view of the consequences of different gender strategies – prosperity and poverty, dominance and dependence. Above all, Moodie gives us a sense of the complex but powerful processes of historical change that transform gender arrangements over time.

Case 3: Bending gender

In the early 1980s a new and devastating disease was identified, eventually named 'AIDS' (acquired immune deficiency syndrome). It was soon shown to be connected with a virus (human immunodeficiency virus, HIV) that killed humans indirectly, by destroying their immune systems' capacity to resist other diseases.

The global HIV/AIDS epidemic has called out a massive research response, from the biological studies which defined HIV – but have yet to produce a vaccine – to studies of the sexual practices in which infection is mainly transmitted. The commonest form of 'behavioural' research, as it is usually called in health studies, is survey research using questionnaires. But research of that kind, though it yields useful counts of episodes, gives limited understanding of the meanings that sexual encounters have for the partners, their place in the lives of the people involved.

It is precisely that kind of understanding that is crucial for AIDS prevention strategies – which, to be successful, must involve people in protecting themselves. Therefore some researchers have turned to more sensitive and open-ended research strategies. One of the most notable products of this approach is Gary Dowsett's *Practicing Desire* (1996). This Australian study uses a traditional sociological method, the oral life-history, to create a vivid and moving portrait of homosexual sex in the era of AIDS.

Dowsett's study is based on interviews with twenty men. This may seem like a small number. But good life-history research is remarkably complex, produces a tremendous volume of evidence and a lot of theoretical leads, and cannot be hurried. Dowsett's study took nine years to get from first interviews to final publication. Each of the twenty respondents gave a narrative of his life, talked in intimate detail about relationships and sexual practices, discussed the communities he lived in, his jobs and workplaces, his relations with the wider world, and his connections with the HIV/AIDS epidemic. The evidence is remarkably rich, and raises important questions about gender (among other issues). It is so rich, indeed, that I will discuss just one of the participants here.

Huey Brown, better known as Harriet, was in his late thirties at the time of the interviews. He is a well-known figure in the homosexual networks of an urban working-class community, 'Nullangardie', which has been proletarian (in Moodie's sense) for generations. His father was a truck driver, his mother a housewife. He left school at fourteen, and went to work at the checkout of a local supermarket. He has held a succession of unskilled jobs, mostly in cafes or hotels; he currently works as a sandwich maker. He doesn't have much money or education and has no professional certificate in anything. But Harriet is a formidable AIDS educator, not only organizing and fund-raising for AIDS-related events, but also being an informal teacher of safe sex and an influential community mentor.

Harriet became involved in homosexual sex in adolescence, not as a result of any identity crisis or alignment with a 'gay community' (which hardly existed there at the time), simply by engaging in informal and pleasurable erotic encounters with other boys and with men. Dowsett points out that homosexuality does not necessarily exist as a well-defined 'opposite' to heterosexuality. Among the boys and men of Nullangardie there are many sexual encounters and sexual networks which never get named, yet make an important part of sexuality as it really is.

Harriet is an enthusiast for sex, has had a very large number of partners, is skilful in many sexual techniques, adopts different positions in different sexual encounters, and gets diverse (and perverse) responses from different partners. As Dowsett remarks, this kind of evidence – by no means confined to Harriet's case – undermines any doctrine that there is a single, standard pattern of male sexuality.

Like many other people, Harriet wanted stable relationships, and has had three. The first was with a jealous man who beat him severely; the third was with a pre-operative transsexual, which was hurtful in other ways. The second, with Jim, the love of Harriet's life, lasted nine years. 'It was a husband and wife team sort of thing. I looked after him and he looked after me.' Jim took the penetrative role in sex, 'He was that straight that he just didn't like a cock near his bum.' Jim worked in the building trade, they lived together, they baby-sat Jim's nieces and nephews, and some of Jim's family accepted the relationship quite well.

Still, Harriet was no conventional wife. And as Dowsett remarks, what are we to make of Jim?

It sounds like an ordinary suburban life, except that his partner is a drag queen with breast implants and a penchant for insertive anal intercourse with casual partners on the odd occasion! ... Whatever Jim was or is, he certainly cannot be called 'gay,' and when Harriet says: 'He [Jim] was that straight!' he means a sexually conventional male, not a heterosexually identified one. (1996: 94)

Yet after nine years Jim left Harriet – for a sixteen-year-old girl. There are gender practices here, but not gender boxes – the reality keeps escaping from the orthodox categories.

In some ways the most spectacular escape from the box was becoming a drag queen. In his late teens Huey began to hang out in a cross-dressing scene and became Harriet, working as a 'show girl'. There is a local tradition of drag entertainment involving mime, lip-synch singing, stand-up comedy and striptease. Harriet learnt the techniques of being a 'dragon', was good enough to pass as a woman on occasion, and even had operations to get breast implants. He acquired the camp style of humour and self-presentation which was part of the local tradition. Harriet now uses these techniques, and the local celebrity they gave him, for AIDS fundraising. But he notes a generational change. The younger men, more 'gay' identified than 'camp', now like beefy male strippers better than the old-style drag shows.

Hotel work and drag shows do not pay well, and in a de-industrializing economy the economic prospects of unskilled workers are not good. In his late twenties Harriet tried another form of work, prostitution. He worked in drag, and evidently many of his customers presumed he was a woman. Some knew the score, or suspected, and for them his penis became part of the attraction. Harriet did some brothel work, but mostly worked independently on the street.

As Wendy Chapkis (1997) shows in a recent US/Dutch study, there are tremendous variations in the situations that sex workers face and in their level of control over the work. Harriet was right at one end of the spectrum, remaining firmly in control. He did not use narcotics, he offered only certain services, and he insisted on safe sex. He was skilful in sexual technique, and acquired loyal customers, some of whom stayed with him after he retired from the street – and after he took off the frocks. Even so, there was risk in street work, and a price to pay. Harriet learned to keep constantly aware of where the client's hands were. After several years and two arrests, he gave it up. Even so, his sexual reputation stayed with him, and on this account he was refused a job as an outreach worker with a local AIDS service organization.

Harriet's story (of which this is the barest outline) constantly calls into question the conventional categories of gender. It is not just that Harriet crosses gender boundaries. He certainly did that, with ingenuity and persistence, as a drag artist, surgical patient, wife, prostitute and activist. Yet Harriet is a man, not a transsexual male-becoming-female, and has mostly lived as a man. (In recognition of that, Dowsett writes, and I have followed his example, 'Harriet . . . he'.) The gender perplexity is also a question of Harriet's partners, customers, and social milieu. Every element in the story seems to be surging beyond the familiar categories.

Dowsett argues that the categories of gender analysis are seriously inadequate to understand what is going on here. He mentions critiques of gender theory for being 'heterosexist', preoccupied with heterosexual relations and unable to understand people who are not heterosexual. He suggests gender categories are often used in a mechanical and unrealistic way; in his research, gender identity does not determine sexual practice. Even when gender terms are used, in the context of homosexual sex they are transformed; an example is Harriet's comment on 'husband and wife'.

Sexual desire and practice thus seem to act like a powerful acid dissolving familiar categories:

> But Harriet also teaches us that these gender categories are subject to deconstruction in sex itself: some like being penetrated by a fully frocked transsexual; some clients eventually do not need the drag at all; pleasure and sensation, fantasy and fixation, are the currency in a sexual economy where the sexed and gendered bodies rather than determining the sexual engagement *desire* to lend themselves to even further disintegration. (Dowsett 1996: 117)

Dowsett thus raises the question of the limits of gender analysis, and questions the concept of gender identity. It is clear that gender is *present* in most of the episodes of Harriet's life. But it is also clear that gender does not *fix* Harriet's (or his partners') sexual practices. Sometimes gender seems to provide the raw material for processing, rather than the finished product. Harriet's work as a drag artist, for instance, rested on gender categories and conventions familiar to his audiences; these conventions are parodied and jokingly reproduced in the performance. Nevertheless Harriet's work as a prostitute, with all its gender ambiguities, rested on a gendered economy in Nullangardie which put money in the pockets of his clients – all of them men. Equally their practice as clients rested on a masculine culture which regarded men as entitled to sexual gratification.

One of the lessons of this research is that we cannot treat gender relations as a mechanical system. If human action is creative – as all three of these studies show – we are always moving into historical spaces that no one has occupied before. At the same time we do not create in a vacuum. We act in particular situations created by our own, and other people's, past actions. As shown by Harriet's complex sexual improvisations on materials provided by the gender order, we work on the past as we move into the future.

Case 4: Women, war and memory

One of the great experiments in gender equality was undertaken by the Soviet Union. The communist government established after the Russian revolutions of 1917, and the bitter civil war that followed, was formally committed to equal rights for women. A prominent feminist, Alexandra Kollontai, was minister for social welfare in the first Soviet government. A major investment was made in girls' and women's education, women's health services and childcare facilities. Women's participation in industry and other forms of technical employment rose to levels never matched in the capitalist 'West'. The regime claimed to have achieved equality between women and men, and open access for women to all spheres of social and public life.

At the end of the 1980s the system that held these ideals collapsed with stunning speed. In the countries that emerged from the former Soviet Union, different ideas about gender also emerged. Irina Novikova (2000: 119) notes how the attempt to create a new national identity for the post-Soviet regime in Latvia involved an appeal to surprisingly archaic models of gender:

> This started with a 'return to the past', to the patriarchal traditions embedded in the paternalist and authoritarian model of the state that existed before Soviet annexation in 1939 . . . In this process, men were supposed to reorganize the state, while women/mothers were supposed to enshrine the 'umbilical' role of a cultural gatekeeper within the family/home/nation/state.

What happened in Latvia appears to have happened in most post-Soviet regimes, including Russia itself, and the former Yugoslavia

(Slapšak 2000). They are openly dominated by men, they marginalize women, and they weave together their nation-building with an aggressive masculinity that at times spills over into a warrior ideology. It is, on the face of it, a stunning historical reversal – from a system of gender equality to a militant, misogynist patriarchy. Why has this occurred?

Novikova, by profession a literary critic and historian, offers a fascinating answer in her recent essay 'Soviet and post-Soviet masculinities: after men's wars in women's memories'. This is an impressive example of the cultural analysis of gender, an approach that raises questions not about individual lives, or particular institutional settings, but about the broad cultural meanings of gender and the way those meanings frame individual experience.

Novikova argues that the reassertion of local patriarchies was fuelled by the desire to reject the Soviet experiment as a whole.

> It is commonly believed that men were emasculated, made effeminate, by the official Soviet model of sex equality. It is popularly believed that men's historic identity was lost, and now has to be restored. Thus the critical response to the failure of the whole Soviet utopian project is reflected in a gender dynamic. In the arguments of post-Soviet nationalist and conservative state rebuilding, the essential falseness of the utopian project is proved by the fact that it attributed feminine features to men and masculine features to women, thus reversing the 'natural' sex roles. (2000: 119)

This reaction is reinforced by the precarious position of the new regimes. They are poor and dependent economies in a global capitalism dominated by the West. The celebration of a strong, competitive masculinity can be seen as a means of adjusting to this new, hostile and potentially overwhelming environment. Hence new (though also quite archaic) cults of military masculinity, and the rapid emergence of the myth of the hypermasculine Russian Mafia.

So far, the story seems straightforward; but it is more complicated than that. As Novikova also points out, the reassertion of masculine privilege could hardly have gone so well if the Soviet system had really been as egalitarian as it claimed, if women had really been in a position of equal power with men.

Stalin's regime was not just a brutal dictatorship, it was a dictatorship that specialized in egalitarian lies. Under the progressive facade of 'communism' lived a system of inequality, perhaps not as spectacular as the inequalities of capitalism but certainly as deeply entrenched. Part of this was a structure of gender inequality. Many of the gains women made at the Revolution were rolled back in subsequent decades, for instance abortion rights. Women won a higher proportion of seats in Soviet parliaments than in almost any other part of the world – but the Soviet parliaments had no power. In the bodies that held real power (for instance the central executive of the communist party) women were a small minority. Women were present in the paid economy, certainly, but they also did most of the unpaid housework and childcare.

Yet, Novikova points out, women had an important symbolic place in Soviet Russian culture, which derived from earlier periods of Russian history. This was a place as *mother*, especially as mother to sons. The regime put a lot of energy into reconciling the needs of women as workers with their role as mothers. But it also drew on powerful cultural themes about maternity. Indeed there was a level at which woman-as-mother was symbolically identified with Russia itself, sending forth sons-as-soldiers to liberate the world. A gendered myth of war was created which grew to full flower in the Second World War and still existed when the regime tried to justify its military intervention in Afghanistan in the 1980s.

But women's actual experiences might be very different from the role in which women were cast by the regime. To explore this issue, Novikova turns to a little-discussed genre, women's war memoirs. She discusses the work of two writers. For lack of space I will skip over Elena Rzhevskaya (author of *Distant Rumble*, personally involved in one of the most dramatic moments of the Second World War, the search for Hitler in 1945), to concentrate on the more recent writer, Svetlana Alexievich.

Alexievich is the author of *Zinc Boys*, a controversial book about the 'unknown war' the Soviet regime fought and lost in Afghanistan – and also about Soviet motherhood. The title (which does not translate well) is an ironic allusion, on the one hand to the zinc coffins used by the Soviet army in this war, on the other to the Soviet imagery of 'steel' soldiers and workers in heroic narratives of earlier wars. The regime presented the Afghanistan war too as a crusade for peace and social justice. But it failed, despite superior technology and heavy casualties. Eventually the Soviet forces were thrown out of Afghanistan and the socialist government they supported collapsed. The ultimate victors were the militant misogynists of the Taliban movement who control the country now.

Alexievich interviewed veterans of the war in the 1980s, including women who had been there as military nurses. It is clear that the trauma created by this war was comparable to the failed American war in Vietnam, with similar levels of brutality, horror and doubt. Though the

Soviet regime was more successful at the time in controlling public opposition, it merely drove the trauma underground. *Zinc Boys* opened the wounds again, to the anger both of veterans and of non-participants who wanted to have the whole ghastly mess forgotten.

The book is an attempt at multiple autobiography, in which Alexievich as editor/author both uses and challenges the familiar cultural representation of the mother–son relationship in war. The writer's position is like that of the mother, but also unlike, especially confronting the emotional havoc among the Russian participants in this war. Instead of the welcoming and supportive national/maternal body, Alexievich and her readers confront body-memories of a different kind: male bodies, dead, torn apart, tortured, piled up and waiting for the zinc coffins – which were in short supply.

The memories of defeat and mental devastation, and the powerful image of the war cemetery with unmarked graves, shatters the traditional imagery of the heroic male soldier at war. But the symbolic position of women in relation to this war is also untenable. The code of the strong woman, the amazon, the fighter for a larger cause, is destroyed by women's real memories of harassment, humiliation, and sexual exploitation in the war zone – by the men of their own side. Women's activism – participation in the crusade – simply made them vulnerable to exploitation, tearing up romantic dreams of marriage and love.

Returning from the war, women found this experience impossible to reconcile with the cultural expectations for womanhood, with the model of a virtuous worker-wife. The only way to handle the contradiction was to erase the memory. Hence some of the outrage created by Alexievich's text, which contested this erasure.

The men returning from the war turned in another direction. For them, the failed war had been an experience of collective impotency. After the American defeat in Vietnam, as a gripping study by Susan Jeffords (1989) has shown, American films and novels put a lot of energy into the reassertion of men's potency and authority vis-à-vis a more available target: local women, and the fiction of sex equality. Novikova shows the parallel in the Soviet Union: 'Women are reminded that the masquerade is over, that equality was only a gift, and that female warriors are not to transgress the normal, biologically prescribed confines of their sex' (2000: 128).

Women's memoirs, Novikova argues, unveil the hidden gender dynamics beneath the facade of Soviet equality – and this helps us understand the post-Soviet shift away from the commitment to gender equality. Especially this helps us understand why it is often women themselves who support this shift. Having been through these traumas they want 'only the right to forget their activism', and many become staunch proponents of the new patriarchy and the image of a powerful man. Thus we can gain an understanding of the – sometimes paradoxical – gender patterns in post-Soviet life by a careful attention to cultural history, to the ways traditional gender orders were both preserved and transformed in the Soviet era of 'sex equality'.

Other recent and notable studies might have been included in this chapter; more will be mentioned in later chapters. These four cases are, however, enough to show the diversity of gender dynamics, their complexity, and their power. In talking about 'gender' we are not talking about simple differences or fixed categories. We are talking about relationships, boundaries, practices, identities and images that are actively created in social processes, come into existence in specific historical circumstances, shape the lives of people in profound and often contradictory ways, and are subject to historical struggle and change. How to reconcile this complexity with the familiar dichotomy of male and female bodies will be the subject of the next chapter.

3

Differences and Bodies

At the centre of common-sense thinking about gender is the idea of difference between women and men. When pop psychologists tell us that women are naturally more emotional than men, or that our lives are ruled by 'brain sex', or that boys fight and steal cars because of testosterone, they are appealing to familiar beliefs about sex differences, especially bodily differences. In this chapter I will examine ideas and evidence about this question, and at the end I will suggest a more helpful way of thinking about bodies and gender than is usually found in discussions of difference.

Reproductive difference

Why is there any difference at all between women's and men's bodies? Humans share with many other species, plants as well as animals, the system of sexual reproduction – a method of reproducing which allows genetic information from two individuals to be combined, rather than just one to be copied. Sexual reproduction is itself a product of evolution, perhaps 400 million years old. Life forms existed earlier, reproducing in other ways – as many species still do. Some, including orchids and grasses, reproduce both sexually and asexually. Biologists debate why sex evolved, for this odd scheme has some evolutionary disadvantages. It may have evolved because sexual reproduction allows faster change, or prevents the accumulation of harmful mutations.

Sexual reproduction does not require bodies to be specialized by sex. Among earthworms, for instance, each individual is hermaphrodite, producing both sperm and ova (eggs), and thus every worm is able to perform both male and female functions. In other groups individuals produce either sperm or ova but not both. Their bodies are to some extent 'dimorphic', that is, in a given species there exist two forms. Humans are among these species.

Genetic information is encoded in DNA and carried on chromosomes, microscopic structures within the nucleus of each cell in a plant or animal. The genetic information that is combined at fertilization (in sexual reproduction) comes half from a female, in the egg nucleus, and half from a male, in the sperm nucleus. Human cells have forty-six chromosomes, which come in pairs. One pair, the sex chromosomes, influences the development of the body's male and female sexual characteristics. Women have two X chromosomes, men have one X and one Y chromosome, in this pair. Under the influence of the genetic information here, male and female bodies develop specialized organs – wombs, testes, breasts – and certain differences in physiology, such as the balance of hormones circulating in the blood, and the menstrual cycle in women.

Among mammals, females not only produce ova but also carry foetuses in a protective womb (except for monotremes such as the platypus, which lay eggs), and then feed infants with milk from specialized organs (in humans, breasts). Among some mammal species, but not all, males have extra bulk, or extra equipment: the antlers of male deer, for instance. Humans are mammals with well-differentiated reproductive systems, but modest physical differences between sexes in other respects. We do not have antlers.

In several respects human bodies are not fully dimorphic. First, there is a complex group of intersex categories, such as females lacking a second X chromosome, males with an extra X chromosome, and others. These categories have long fascinated sexologists, and do not correspond in any simple way to behaviour. The biologist Anne Fausto-Sterling (2000: 51) estimates that intersex groups, taken together, may account for 1.7 per cent of all births: a small but not trivial number.

Second, physical differences between male and female change over the lifespan. In the early stages of development male and female bodies are relatively undifferentiated; there are only small differences between a two-year old girl and a two-year-old boy. Even the obviously different external reproductive organs – penis, clitoris, scrotum and labia – develop embryonically from a common starting point. In a number of respects male and female bodies also become more similar in old age.

Third, even in early adulthood the physical characteristics of males as a group, and females as a group, overlap extensively. Height is a simple example. Adult males are on average a little taller than adult females, but the diversity of heights within each group is great, in relation to the average difference. Therefore many individual women are taller than many individual men. A more complex example is the brain – the site of a great deal of discussion of sex differences in recent years. There are some differences in brain anatomy and functioning between women and men, for instance in the tendency to use particular areas of the brain in language processing. But the differences are fewer, and less reliably established, than aggressive popular accounts of 'brain sex' would suggest. In many areas of brain anatomy and functioning there are no significant sex differences; and where there are differences, there is also common ground. As the neuroscientist Lesley Rogers (2000: 34) puts it: 'The brain does not choose neatly to be either a female or a male type. In any aspect of brain function that we can measure there is considerable overlap between females and males.' As we shall see, this is also a key point about human behaviour.

Ideas of difference

The fact of reproductive difference between male and female humans is not controversial, but its significance is. On this question, approaches to gender diverge sharply. I will outline the three most influential: the idea of natural difference, which treats the body as a machine; the idea of two separate realms of sex and gender; and the idea of gender as a discursive or symbolic system, which treats bodies as a canvas on which society paints.

The body as machine

In many discussions of gender, reproductive difference is assumed to be directly reflected in a whole range of other differences: bodily strength and speed (men are stronger and faster), physical skills (men have mechanical skills, women are good at fiddly work), sexual desire (men have more powerful urges), recreational interests (men love sport, women gossip), character (men are aggressive, women are nurturant), intellect (men are rational, women have intuition), and so on. It is widely believed that these differences are large, and that they are 'natural'.

The idea that natural difference provides the basis for the social pattern of gender takes many forms. The nineteenth-century philosopher

John Stuart Mill, in a famous essay entitled *The Subjection of Women*, assumed that men's dominance in society was an expression of greater physical strength. More up-to-date is the idea that men dominate because, with their higher levels of testosterone, they have a hormonal 'aggression advantage' in competition for top jobs. Therefore society needs patriarchy – Steven Goldberg claims in *Why Men Rule* (1993) – to protect women from failure, and to ensure the smooth functioning of institutions.

More complex versions of the argument have been proposed by the US biologist Edward Wilson, who coined the term 'sociobiology', and a group of psychologists who have taken up Wilson's ideas and call their work 'evolutionary psychology'. Broadly, these arguments deduce social gender from reproductive strategies. Assuming that human behaviour is partly inherited, the Darwinian process of natural selection will favour those behaviours which increase the survival rates of any individual's genes into the next generation. From this starting point theorists have deduced human kinship loyalties, mothers' commitment to their children, husbands' sexual infidelity, women's coyness, men's interest in pornography, male bonding, and a remarkable range of other gender patterns (Degler 1990).

An admirable, detailed presentation of the 'evolutionary psychology' argument on gender is given by David Geary in *Male, Female* (1998). Geary's aim is to link psychological research on sex differences with the concept of 'sexual selection' (the choice of mates in sexual reproduction) as a mechanism of evolution. After expounding biological research on sexual selection in other species, Geary works his way through the now huge research literature on human sex differences (see below). For each topic where a sex difference can be located, Geary offers an account of how it might be linked to sexual selection, that is, how humans choose, win and control mates.

Models of the body as a machine producing gender difference are mainly advanced by men, and have often been used to defend the existing gender order, to ridicule feminism or (in Geary's case) feminist ideas of 'gender roles'. Sociobiological ideas about innate difference are often presented as the scientific 'truth' about gender, which feminists deny and which societies violate at their peril. However, there are also feminist arguments which present bodies as direct sources of gender difference. Western feminists in the 1980s often saw male aggression and female peacefulness as natural. The terms 'male violence' and 'male sexuality', which became common at this time, implicitly linked behaviour to the body, and some activists directly identified the penis as the source of male power (a view discussed in Segal 1994).

The idea of natural difference runs into difficulties on several fronts. Sociobiological explanations of human kinship, for instance, foundered when the predictions from genetics failed to match the realities of kinship systems actually documented by anthropologists (Sahlins 1977). It seems that social logic works independently of genetic logic. The explanation of gender hierarchy by a hormonal 'aggression advantage' founders when it is discovered that higher testosterone levels *follow from* social dominance as much as they precede it (Kemper 1990).

Geary's argument, being recent and sophisticated, is particularly worth attention. Geary's account of sexual selection is based on individuals making choices that maximize their genetic payoff, very like firms in a free market maximizing their utilities in neo-classical economic models. Geary can't really 'see' society as a reality, so his arguments don't have any place for institutionalized gender arrangements. For instance, in discussing the higher levels of violence among men than among women, all he can see is male vs male competition for reproductive resources; he cannot see military institutions, collective struggles, gendered interests or cultural definitions of manhood and womanhood. It is characteristic of this literature that Geary speaks constantly of 'males' and 'females', not 'men' and 'women'.

Lacking any account of social process, Geary constantly falls back on evolutionary speculation to explain the facts of social life. It comes as a slight shock, after reading this 400-page monograph calling on the name of science and published by so august an institution as the American Psychological Association, to realize that the entire argument is speculation. Not one sex difference in psychological characteristics has actually been *shown* to result from evolutionary mechanisms.

Theodore Kemper (1990) argues that we need to replace the idea of natural difference with a more complex chain of social–biological–social causation. Body-machine models of gender assume that the machine runs by itself: that biological causation is independent of society. But there have been no human (or even hominid) bodies outside society for a very long time. Social processes can be traced for 2.5 million years, give or take a few weeks. (This is the approximate age of the earliest hand-tool cultures so far discovered by archaeologists (Semaw 2000). The discovery of such industries proves the social transmission of specific techniques for making stone tools, over this length of time.)

It is clear that bodies are affected by social processes. Health, child development, and sport provide abundant proof. The way our bodies grow and function is influenced by food distribution, sexual customs, warfare, work, urbanization, education and medicine, to name only the most obvious influences. And *all* these influences are structured by gender. So we cannot think of social gender arrangements as just following from the properties of bodies. They also precede bodies, form the conditions in which bodies develop and live. There is, as Celia Roberts (2000) puts it, a co-construction of the biological and the social.

A further problem with body-machine arguments concerns the way we create scientific knowledge about difference. Two decades ago a brilliant analysis by the ethnomethodologists Suzanne Kessler and Wendy McKenna (1978) showed how much is taken for granted. The literature of research on sex differences rests on attributions of gender. In sex difference research, 'sex' is almost never tested biologically. Rather, the subjects are sorted into 'male' and 'female' by common-sense *social* judgements, as the investigators set up their experiments.

The historical research of Thomas Laqueur (1990) has shown that scientific perceptions of bodily differences change over time. The presumption that human bodies fall into two opposed, qualitatively different, types became general only in the nineteenth century. Earlier it was presumed that male and female bodies were more and less developed versions of one type. Neither view is forced on us by unequivocal evidence. It is a matter of what we presume and therefore what we 'see' when we look at a complex reality.

The widespread idea that testosterone is a 'male hormone' is the most popular current example of presumed dichotomy. Testosterone is, in fact, present in all human bodies. So is the 'female hormone' oestrogen. As Lesley Rogers (2000) points out, many women have higher levels of testosterone in their bloodstream than many men, and after age fifty, men on average have higher levels of oestrogen in their bloodstream than women. Judith Butler persuasively argues in *Gender Trouble* (1990) that the Western belief in 'opposite sexes' is a projection of the modern Western cultural pattern of heterosexual couples onto the natural world. We project this onto other species as well as our own.

The two realms

In the 1970s a number of theorists proposed a sharp distinction between 'sex' and 'gender'. Sex was the biological fact, the difference between the male and the female human animal. Gender was the social fact, the difference between masculine and feminine roles, or men's and women's personalities.

To many at the time, this distinction was a conceptual breakthrough. It cut the knot of natural difference, and showed why biology could not be used to justify women's subordination. The effects of biological difference could be confined to the realm of biology itself. A broad realm of the social ('culture', 'roles', etc.) remained, where gender as we experience it was constructed. This was a realm of freedom, where individuals or societies could choose the gender patterns they wanted. Thus Eleanor Maccoby and Carol Jacklin, the authors of a vast and influential survey of *The Psychology of Sex Differences* (1975), concluded:

> We suggest that societies have the option of minimizing, rather than maximizing, sex differences through their socialization practices. A society could, for example, devote its energies more toward moderating male aggression than toward preparing women to submit to male aggression, or toward encouraging rather than discouraging male nurturance activities.

The concept of 'androgyny' put forward by Sandra Bem (1974) and other psychologists at this time was a widely popular attempt to define an alternative gender pattern, a mixture of masculine and feminine characteristics, which an individual or a society could choose.

The 'sex vs. gender' formula obviously derives from the familiar 'body vs. mind' distinction in Western philosophy. This helped make it acceptable. At the high tide of American liberal feminism in the 1970s, the two-realms model supported an optimistic, even sunny, view of change. Oppressive gender arrangements, being the products of past choices, could be abolished by fresh choices. In the language of the day, sex role expectations could be altered, and sex role socialization would follow suit.

Whole reform agendas were constructed around this principle. Among them were media reforms (to change sex role models), educational reforms (to change the expectations transmitted to girls and boys), and new forms of psychotherapy (to help individuals make the change to new roles). A notable example is the pioneering Australian Schools Commission's report *Girls, School and Society* (1975). This described the ways girls were held back by restrictive social stereotypes, and proposed action to break down educational segregation and widen girls' choices beyond the narrow band of conventional 'women's jobs' such as secretarial work. From this report flowed a series of projects encouraging girls to work in areas such as mathematics, science and technology.

The two-realms model, however, soon ran into trouble, as Rosemary Pringle (1992) shows in a careful critique. The idea of gender as culturally chosen difference ('sex roles') was unable to explain why one side of that difference, the masculine, was consistently more highly valued than the other. The separation of gender from bodies ran counter to developments in feminism which were placing stronger emphasis on bodies. These developments included the growing concern with men's violence and heterosexual sexuality, whose target is not a feminine role but women's bodies; and the growing influence of French theorists who highlighted bodies as the objects of social power and the sources of emotion and symbolism. Some feminist philosophers influenced by this school (e.g. Elizabeth Grosz 1994) insist there is no consistent distinction between body and mind, and that our embodiment itself is adequate to explain our subjectivity.

If the two realms cannot be held strictly apart, perhaps they can be added? A common-sense compromise would suggest that gender differences arise from *both* biology and social norms.

This additive conception underlies most discussions of gender in social psychology, where the term 'sex role' is still widely used. This very phrase adds together a biological and a dramaturgical term. Similarly, moderate sociobiologists (e.g. Degler 1990) assume that there is some social elaboration of the biological differences they believe in: for instance, that boys' natural aggressiveness is socially channelled into football, war, or peanut marketing.

There are difficulties in the additive conception too. For one thing, the two levels of analysis are not really comparable. It is almost always assumed that the biology is fundamental. Biology's reality is more real than sociology's, its explanations are more powerful, and its categories are fixed. To take just one example (though a particularly telling one), the passage from Maccoby and Jacklin quoted above continues:

> In our view, social institutions and social practices are not merely reflections of the biologically inevitable. A variety of social institutions are viable within the framework set by biology. It is up to human beings to select those that foster the life styles they most value.

Maccoby and Jacklin argue for social choice, and want change, but the causal priority in their analysis is clear. Biology determines; only within its 'framework' may humans choose their social arrangements. Sex role theory and sex difference research constantly collapse into biological dichotomy. It is striking that the same collapse occurs in the 'corporeal feminism' of Grosz. Bodies, to Grosz, are either male or female, so the corporeal subjectivity she outlines is necessarily sex-specific – either female or male.

Another key problem in adding social to biological differences is that the patterns of difference at the two levels need not match. Claims about 'sex dimorphism in behaviour' reflect popular ideology rather than reality. As we have seen already, human bodies are dimorphic only in limited ways. On the other side, human behaviour is hardly dimorphic at all, even in areas closely related to sexual reproduction. For instance, while few men do childcare with infants, it is also true that, at any given time, most women are not doing this work either. There are strong gender patterns in childcare, but they do not take the shape of a dichotomy between all-women and all-men. As I will show below, in traits like aggression and intellectual skill there is huge overlap between the two groups.

Not even the categories need match. In different contexts, the social process may define one gender ('unisex' fashion), two genders (Hollywood movies), three genders (many North American native cultures), or four genders (nineteenth-century European urban society once 'homosexuals' and 'lesbians' were sorted out). In current social life there is a whole spectrum of gender variations. These have been painstakingly catalogued by Judith Lorber in *Paradoxes of Gender* (1994). She calculates that modern Western societies distinguish five sexes (including intersexes), three sexual orientations, five gender displays, six types of relationships, and ten self-identifications. Leaving aside the five sexes, that makes, if my arithmetic is correct, 900 different gender situations one can be in. So much for 'dimorphism'.

There are times when, as additive theories propose, social processes do elaborate on bodily difference. The Wonderbra springs to mind. But there are other times when social process distorts, contradicts, complicates, minimizes or modifies bodily difference. As Thorne's study (chapter 2 above) shows, the social process in an elementary school may do several of these things in turn, in the course of an ordinary day.

For multiple reasons, then, it is impossible to sustain either version of the two-realms model of gender. Perhaps we have to look to the social realm exclusively to account for gender difference. In cultural analysis there are approaches which examine bodies as surfaces to be written on ('inscribed'), or canvases to be painted.

The body as canvas

Second-wave feminism from the start was concerned with the way women's bodies were represented and, as images, consumed. One of the first Women's Liberation demonstrations was against the 'Miss America' beauty pageant at Atlantic City in 1968. Research on gender imagery is one of the great accomplishments of Women's Studies as an academic field. Historical research such as Lois Banner's *American Beauty* (1983) traces the shifting but powerful systems of signs through which women's bodies are defined as elegant, beautiful and desirable, or unfashionable and ugly. *The Politics of Women's Bodies* (Weitz 1998), a recent collection, shows how the analysis has been extended across diversities of race, class and sexuality, and into issues such as surgery and sport.

Analyses of the imagery of women's bodies in film, television, photography and other visual arts have reached high levels of sophistication, and have fed into mainstream art criticism. An excellent example is *Modern Boy Modern Girl* (Menzies 1998), an art show which traced the interplay between the modernist movement in early twentieth-century Japan, and gender changes in the new urban culture. This period saw the emergence of a new individualism and the images of 'mobo' and 'moga' (modern boy and modern girl) in Tokyo. As the 'modern boy' story shows, the approach can be applied to men's bodies as well as women's. Anthony Easthope showed in *What a Man's Gotta Do* (1986) how men's bodies are symbolized as masculine in the imagery of Western advertising, film, and news reports.

Recent cultural studies of the body often focus on language or discourse, under the influence of Michel Foucault. In a number of historical studies, most completely in *Discipline and Punish* (1977), Foucault showed how modern systems of knowledge sort people into categories, and how these categories are interwoven with techniques of social discipline that police their bodies. A key role is played by professions such as medicine, psychology and criminology that apply these techniques. Bodies have been watched and controlled in finer and finer detail, as 'power-knowledge' became more sophisticated, the professions that apply it become larger and more numerous, and the institutions in which it operates, such as factories, prisons and schools, extended their grip on Western societies. Foucault's line of thought has been generalized in the sociology of the body developed by Bryan Turner (1984) and others. Turner proposes the concept of 'body practices', observing that 'bodies are objects over which we labour – eating, sleeping, cleaning, dieting, exercising'.

Foucault, notoriously, failed to theorize gender (though most of his stuff is actually about men in masculinized institutions). However, his approach was taken up by many feminists (e.g. Fraser 1989), and is readily turned into a theory of gender by treating gendered bodies as the products of disciplinary practices. The effects are material; the canvas has real marks placed on it. In modern society, biology bends to the hurricane of social discipline. Bodies are 'docile'; difference is produced by disciplinary practice.

Field research shows how the 'disciplining' is done. The Los Angeles body-building gyms studied by the ethnographer Alan Klein (1993) show a whole sub-culture of men subjected to a fierce regime of exercise, diet and drugs. Over years of subjection to this regime their bodies are sculpted into the ideal masculine forms desired in body-building competitions. This may be an extreme case, but more moderate disciplining of bodies is very widespread. It is undertaken by such large-scale institutions as sport, education and medicine. The introduction of 'physical training' in public school systems, traced in Australia by David Kirk (1993) and in the Netherlands by Mineke van Essen (2000), created schemes for training boys' and girls' bodies differently. Modern physical education is interwoven with competitive sport, and there is now impressive documentation of the gendered character of sports institutions. Nancy Theberge (1991) clearly shows how the different exercise regimes for men and women, the disciplinary practices that both teach and constitute sports, are designed to produce gendered bodies.

And if social discipline cannot produce gendered bodies, the knife can. Cosmetic surgery is now big business; bodies are literally carved to the shape prescribed by gender symbolism. The silicon breast implant scandal has made public the scale on which this has been done in the United States, where big breasts are thought sexy. This whole industry, one might think, flies in the face of the ideology of natural difference. Research on cosmetic surgeons and their clients by Diana Dull and Candace West (1991) shows a startling solution to this violation. Apparently cosmetic surgery is now considered 'natural' for a woman, but not for a man. The exception is penile surgery, where penis enlargement is now a considerable business.

Body-canvas approaches, though they have been wonderfully productive, also run into difficulty. The approach emphasizes the 'signifier' to the point where the 'signified' practically vanishes. With gender, the difficulty is crucial. What makes a symbolic structure a gender structure, rather than some other kind, is the fact that its signs refer, directly or indirectly, to the reproductive relationship between women and men.

This is not to say that all gender relations are reproductive, in the sense that they produce children. Far from it – even when they directly involve sex. Most heterosexual sexuality does not result in pregnancy, and homosexual relations too are gendered. As Rosemary Pringle (1992: 91) commented, 'Whether you went to bed with a man or a woman continued to matter!' Gender involves a lot more than one-to-one relation-ships between bodies; it involves a vast and complicated institutional and cultural order. It is this whole order that comes into relation with bodies, and gives them gender meanings.

Post-structuralist theory acknowledges that order, but often exagger-ates the docility of bodies. Bodies may participate in disciplinary regimes not because they are docile, but because they are active. They seek pleas-ure, seek experience, seek transformation. Some startling examples of this can be found in contemporary SM (sadomasochist) sexual subcul-tures. People submit to corsets, chains, piercing, branding, rope bondage, and a whole spectrum of painfully restrictive clothes in rubber and leather – all voluntarily, indeed with delight, as Valerie Steele shows in *Fetish* (1996). What is seen in extreme form here is surely true, in milder forms, of the whole system of fashion.

Bodies are also recalcitrant and difficult. In *The Men and the Boys* (Connell 2000) I give some case studies of this. One is a young man whose driven performance of masculinity – partying, drinking, screw-ing around, taking cocktails of drugs, etc. – came to an end because the resilience of his body came to an end. Another is a man whose un-athletic body triggered a sense of difference which became sexual difference. The issue is imaginatively explored in Patrick White's tremen-dous novel *The Twyborn Affair* (1979). This story centres on the exper-ience of Eddie/Eudoxia, whose body cannot settle into any of the locations intended for it – as husband, wife, soldier or pastoralist. Bodies are recalcitrant not because of an inchoate 'resistance' but in organized ways. Bodies grow, age, become sick, desire, learn and forget skills, engender and give birth. These are patterned without necessarily being 'disciplined'.

Bodies also labour. This is a material practice in which bodies are deployed and consumed, and gender meanings arise from this material-ity. The point is forcibly made in Mike Donaldson's (1991) account of working-class life in an Australian steel town. The masculinity of indus-trial labour, as defined in this setting, consists in its heaviness, risk and difficulty. These are ways that bodies are consumed: worn down, injured, sometimes destroyed. Yet, as Donaldson remarks, 'the very destruction of the physical site of masculinity, the body, can be a method of attain-ing, demonstrating and perpetuating the socially masculine'. Donaldson's point applies even more forcibly to the business of demonstrating mas-culinity in war.

Bodies cannot be understood as just the objects of social process, whether symbolic or disciplinary. They are active participants in social process. They participate through their capacities, development and needs, through the friction of their recalcitrance, and through the directions set by their pleasures and skills. Bodies must be seen as sharing in social agency, in generating and shaping courses of social conduct. Yet all the difficulties of biological determinism, outlined above, remain. It seems we need a different way of thinking about bodies and gender, and I will return to this question after considering the evidence on 'sex differences'.

Facts of difference: 'sex similarity' research

Bodily differences and social effects are often linked through the idea of *character dichotomy*. Women are supposed to have one set of traits, men another. Women are supposed to be nurturant, suggestible, talkative, emotional, intuitive, and sexually loyal; men are supposed to be aggressive, tough-minded, taciturn, rational, analytic, and promiscuous. These ideas have been strong in Western culture since the nineteenth century, when the belief that women had weaker intellects and less capacity for judgement than men was used to justify their exclusion from universities and from the vote.

Women have now entered universities and polling-booths, but the belief in character dichotomy remains strong. This is sometimes to women's advantage: for instance, the argument that there should be more women in management and government because they will bring their distinctive traits (e.g. empathy and relationship skills) to these tasks. More often it is to men's advantage: for instance, the belief that women can't be top managers because they lack the necessary aggressiveness and analytical skills; or the belief that when men engage in predatory or selfish sexual conduct they are only doing what is natural for men and cannot be expected to change.

The belief in character dichotomy is so important that it was one of the first issues about gender to be addressed in sustained empirical research. Starting in the 1890s, generations of psychologists have measured various traits with tests or scales, and compared the results for women with those for men. This body of research, long known as 'sex difference' (sometimes 'gender difference') research, is now huge. When Maccoby and Jackson (1975) published their survey of *The Psychology of Sex Differences*, they included more than 1,400 separate studies; and that was on top of another massive compilation, *The Development of Sex Differences*, published a few years earlier (Maccoby 1966). Probably at least as many new studies have been published in the quarter-century since. 'Sex difference' is one of the most-researched topics in psychology. There is also a large parallel literature in sociology and political science, looking in the same way at sex differences in attitudes and opinions, voting, violence and so forth.

The beginning of this research is described in a fascinating historical study by Rosalind Rosenberg, *Beyond Separate Spheres* (1982). The first generation of psychological researchers found, contrary to mainstream Victorian belief, that the mental capacities of men and women were more or less equal. It is an interesting fact that this finding of 'no difference' was rapidly accepted by men as well as women in the mental-testing field. Indeed, as they developed standardized tests of general ability or intelligence (the so-called IQ tests) during the first half of the twentieth century, psychologists incorporated the 'no difference' finding as a given, choosing and scoring test items in such a way that males and females would have equal average scores. Later attempts to find sex differences in this field have come to nothing (Halpern and LaMay 2000). It is now very widely accepted that in general intelligence, there are no significant sex differences.

An even more interesting fact is that *this is the usual finding in the sex difference research as a whole*. In table after table of Maccoby and Jacklin's book, the commonest entry in the column for the finding about difference is 'none'. Study after study, on trait after trait, comparing women's results with men's or girls' with boys', finds no significant difference. In summarizing their findings, the first thing Maccoby and Jacklin (1975: 349) did was list a series of 'Unfounded Beliefs about Sex Differences'. On the evidence they compiled, it is *not* true that girls are more social than boys, that girls are more suggestible than boys, that girls have lower self-esteem, that girls are better at rote learning and boys at higher-level cognitive processing, that boys are more analytic, that girls are more affected by heredity and boys by environment, that girls lack achievement motivation, or that girls are auditory while boys are visual. All these beliefs turn out to be myths.

Maccoby and Jacklin were not alone in this conclusion. Hugh Fairweather (1976), after an extensive examination of the research on sex differences in cognitive skills, concluded that sex differences were too few and uncertain to be worth bothering about. Mark Hogrebe and colleagues (1985), in a very large study of US high school students' reading achievement, concluded that sex differences accounted for just 1 per cent of the variation in scores – compared with 20 per cent accounted for by 'demographic' (social class related) variables. In a recent survey of sex difference research on moral orientation, Sara Jaffee and Janet Hyde (2000) found that 73 per cent of comparisons between men and women on 'care' orientation found no statistically significant difference, and 72 per cent of comparisons on 'justice' orientation found no significant difference. These are just a few examples from many that could be given.

So the overwhelming conclusion from a hundred years of 'sex difference' research is that men and women are not very different at all, across a wide range of traits examined in psychology and related social sciences. To put it more positively, the main finding is that *women and men are psychologically very similar*, as groups. We should long ago have been calling this field 'sex similarity' research. We should have massive tomes on 'The Development of Sex Similarities', conferences on the evolutionary and biological background of sex similarity, and fierce debates on whether nature or nurture best explains the specific sex similarities that have been found.

The psychological similarity of men and women might be regarded, on the volume of evidence supporting it, as one of the best-established generalizations in all the human sciences.

It is therefore intensely interesting to find that this conclusion is widely disbelieved. The acceptance of gender similarity in the field of intelligence testing turns out to have been exceptional. Now pop psychologists, in books selling millions of copies, insist that women and men have different desires, speak different languages, have different capacities and express different attitudes. In the academic world generations of researchers, in the teeth of the evidence their own disciplines have produced, have gone on relentlessly searching for, and writing about, sex differences. The actual tomes, conferences and debates are, of course, about how to explain sex differences, not similarities. The gap between the main pattern actually found, and the widespread belief about what *should* be found, is so great that Cynthia Epstein (1988) entitled her admirable book about dichotomous thinking and gender reality *Deceptive Distinctions*.

Why the reluctance to accept similarity? A large part of the explanation, I am sure, lies in the cultural background. Dichotomous gender symbolism is very strong in Western culture (see chapter 4), so it is not surprising that when researchers (and others) think about sex and gender, what they 'see' is difference. Within our usual mindset and our usual research design, gender similarity is not a positive state; it is merely the absence of proven difference (literally, the 'null hypothesis'). Nature abhors a vacuum, and so do researchers; true difference might always be revealed by improved methods; so, one goes on searching for ever . . . . This way, madness lies.

But there are also more substantial arguments. Conventional psychological tests, it is sometimes said, are too superficial to detect the underlying patterns of gender. The real character differences between women and men may be lodged at a deeper level in personality – say, in the unconscious (as in the currently popular Jungian dichotomy of the 'deep masculine' and the 'deep feminine'). This could be true. Certainly most quantitative tests in psychology measure only the immediately apparent aspects of behaviour, often through self-report. But if the 'deep' differences don't show up at the level of everyday life, and keep on not showing up across a wide range of behaviours – which is what the quantitative research demonstrates – then one wonders how important such deep differences really are. (My opinion is that they too are mythical. Unconscious dynamics are important in understanding human emotion, but they do not fall into a dichotomous pattern.)

A second issue is that the finding of 'no difference' is not uniform. Maccoby and Jacklin also pointed to a small number of traits where sex differences *did* exist, according to the bulk of the evidence: verbal ability, visual-spatial ability, mathematical ability, and aggressiveness. (They entered an open verdict on some other traits, regarding the evidence as inconclusive.) It is these findings, not the 'no difference' findings, which have gone into the textbooks, and have been emphasized and debated by most subsequent writers.

This debate has centered on a third issue. Maccoby and Jacklin had a huge amount of data, but most of it came from hundreds of small studies with ill-defined samples. It may be that the number of 'no difference' findings reflects the methodological weakness of the individual studies. If a way could be found to strengthen the method by combining the results of many studies, the picture might change.

Exactly this became possible when a new statistical procedure, known as 'meta-analysis', was introduced to sex difference research in the 1980s – and was called by some proponents a 'revolution' in the field. The procedure relies on finding a large number of separate studies of the same issue: for instance, many studies attempting to measure sex differences in aggression, or intelligence, or self-esteem. In meta-analysis each study (rather than each person) is taken as one data point, and the task is to make a statistical analysis of the set of studies taken as a group. Obviously before this can be done their findings have to be expressed on a common scale. Unless all the studies have used exactly the same measurement procedures (which in practice is rarely the case), this is a problem. The ingenious solution is to define a common scale based on the variability of individual scores in the original studies.

The usual procedure in sex difference meta-analysis is this. For each study, the difference between the average scores of women and men (on whatever test is being used) is obtained, and this is rewritten as a fraction of the overall variation in people's scores found in that study on that same test. (Technically, the difference between means is divided by the mean within-group standard deviation.) This resembles a familiar way of 'standardizing' scores in psychological measurement. The standardized sex difference, known as 'd', found for each individual study is the measurement taken forward into the meta-analysis. (The convention is that d values above zero indicate that the men's average is higher, values below zero indicate that the women's average is higher.)

In the meta-analysis proper, the d scores for all the studies are examined as a group. An average d score is computed, which is usually called the 'effect size' for that group of studies. A check is made whether the group of d scores is homogeneous – so tightly clustered that probably only one underlying effect is present. If it is not, then the studies can be classified into sub-groups, and statistical checks are run on the influence of 'moderator' variables. For instance, the researcher might check whether the effect size differs between older and newer studies (which might suggest that the size of sex differences is changing over time), or between studies using different tests, or between studies of different age groups, and so on. (There are variations in meta-analytic procedure; for a comprehensive text see Cooper and Hedges 1994.)

The first impact of meta-analysis was to revive confidence in the existence and importance of sex differences generally, as can be seen in Alice Eagly's *Sex Differences in Social Behavior* (1987). Even when many or most studies in a group individually show non-significant sex differences, meta-analysis may find an effect size significantly different from zero in the group as a whole. A few examples from the many effect sizes reported are: +.21 across 216 studies of self-esteem (Kling et al. 1999), –.28 across 160 studies of 'care orientation' in moral choice (Jaffee and Hyde 2000), zero across 22 studies of 'meaning orientation' in learning styles (Severiens and ten Dam 1998), +.48 across 83 studies of aggression (Hyde 1984).

The question then arises, what do these effect sizes mean? An effect may be significantly different from zero (which means it is not a result of pure chance) but may still be so small that it does not tell us much about the world. And here meta-analysis has its limits. By convention, an effect size of .20 is called 'small', .50 is called 'medium', and .80 is called 'large'. But there is no unequivocal way to interpret this convention. Eagly (1987) argues that even small effects may be practically important; but other meta-analysts are less convinced. Kristen Kling and her colleagues (1999) try to get a handle on this issue by comparing their sex difference effect size with the effect sizes that have consequences in other types of research on self-esteem. They conclude that 'the gender difference in self-esteem is small when compared against effect sizes that have been shown to have important consequences in the laboratory'.

As the sex difference research has gone on, and meta-analyses have piled up, there has been a renewed scepticism about the size and universality of sex differences. Maccoby and Jacklin in the 1970s considered that 'verbal ability' was one of the traits where a difference (favouring women) was definitely established. But Hyde and McKinley (1997), reviewing meta-analyses of research since then, report effect sizes clustering around zero. They conclude that 'gender differences with regard to general verbal ability appear to be so small that they are now essentially nonexistent'. Mathematics ability, another claimed area of difference (favouring men), proves to have only a very small effect size, +.15, across 254 studies. Kling et al. (1999: 487) observe that even with a consistent tendency for men's averages to be higher, and a statistically significant effect size of +.21 for sex differences in self-esteem, there is great overlap between women's and men's scores. They note that 'fully 92% of the area under each curve is shared with the other. This substantial overlap of the distributions indicates that males and females are more similar than different on measures of self-esteem'.

Meta-analysis has also increasingly emphasized that sex differences may be specific rather than general. Hyde and McKinley (1997), for instance, though reporting that general verbal ability shows no sex differences, acknowledge that specific language difficulties do reveal gender differences (more boys show difficulties than girls). Science achievement also shows specific patterns. Biology shows no gender difference, while physics shows a persistent difference with an effect size about +.30. Studies of aggression often show a sex difference, as Maccoby and Jacklin reported – but not in all circumstances. Bettencourt and Miller (1996) find an overall *d* of +.22 in experimental studies of aggression, but report that this effect depends on whether or not there are conditions of provocation. Unprovoked, men have a modest tendency to show higher levels of aggressiveness than women (mean effect size +.33); provoked, men's and women's reactions are similar (mean effect size +.17).

A similar method reveals that sex differences in masculinity/femininity, as measured by tests such as the 'Bem Sex Role Inventory', change over time. A meta-analysis by Twenge (1997) finds that men and women (in samples of US undergraduates) became more similar in their responses on these scales over a period of twenty years, from the 1970s to the 1990s. Not, as many people fear, because men are becoming feminized – both groups' scores on the femininity scales changed little. It was rather because the women increased their scores markedly (and men a little) on masculinity scales over this period.

Meta-analysis has not exactly revolutionized the study of sex differences, but it has certainly helped clarify what this body of research is saying. The broad conclusion from earlier research, as summarized by Maccoby and Jacklin, is confirmed. Across a wide range of the traits and characteristics measured by psychology, sharp gender differences are rare. Small differences, or no differences, are common. The concept of character dichotomy, as a basis of gender, is decisively refuted. Broad similarity between women and men is the main pattern.

Meta-analysis adds to this a clearer recognition that specific and situational sex differences often appear. Very specific skills (e.g. in one science rather than another), specific social circumstances (e.g. provocation), specific times and places (e.g. US colleges in the 1990s), and specific ways of measuring traits, all affect the extent of sex differences recorded in the research.

We begin to get a picture of psychological sex differences and similarities, not as fixed, age-old constants of the species, but as the varying products of the active responses people make to a complex and changing social world. In this way, with the aid of meta-analysis, psychology has gradually moved towards the way of understanding gender that has also gradually emerged in sociology.

How far can we generalize from the existing sex similarity research? It is often observed that the modern science of psychology is mainly based on the behaviour of white middle-class students in Psychology 101 courses in US universities – not quite a representative sample of humanity. Given the impressive evidence of cultural and historical variations in gender arrangements (see chapters 2 and 4), we cannot simply assume that the psychological patterns documented for one place and time are also true for others. Yet this very possibility, variation in sex differences between different circumstances, has been emerging as an important conclusion in meta-analytic research. The sex similarity research also includes increasing numbers of large-scale studies with much more adequate samples of the population of Western countries, and some studies in other parts of the world. I think the conclusions outlined above are at least a solid starting point for understanding gender.

Social embodiment

Now that sex similarity research has decisively refuted the concept of character dichotomy, we must reject all models of gender that assume social gender differences to be caused by bodily differences producing character differences. Then how should we understand the relation between body and society in gender?

Bodies have agency *and* bodies are socially constructed. Biological and social analysis cannot be cut apart from each other, as the two-realms model tried to do. But neither can be reduced to the other, as the body-machine and body-canvas models tried to do. Within a 'difference' framework, these conclusions sit as paradoxes. To resolve the paradoxes we must move towards another framework.

'Difference' theories of gender respond to one pattern of bodily difference, the distinction between female and male. Of course there are many other differences among the 6.2 thousand million human bodies in the world. There are large and small, old and young, sick and well, plump and starving. There are skins permanently stained with soil and skins softened with expensive creams; backs ramrod straight and backs stooped over desks and benches; hands cracked from washing and hands spotless and manicured. Each has its trajectory through time, each changes as it grows older. Some bodies encounter accident, traumatic childbirth, violence, starvation, disease or surgery, and have to reorganize themselves to carry on. Some do not survive these encounters.

Yet the tremendous multiplicity of bodies is in no sense a random assortment. The bodies are interconnected through social practices, the things people do in daily life.

Bodies are both objects of social practice and agents in social practice. The same bodies, at the same time, are both. The practices in which bodies are involved form social structures (see chapter 4) and personal trajectories (see chapter 5) which in turn provide the conditions of new practices in which bodies are addressed and involved. There is a loop, a circuit, linking bodily processes and social structures. In fact, there is a tremendous number of such circuits. They occur in historical time, and change over time. They add up to the historical process in which society is embodied, and bodies are drawn into history.

I will call this process *social embodiment*. It might also be seen from the point of view of the body as 'body-reflexive practice', that is, human social conduct in which bodies are both agents and objects.

Bodies are addressed by social processes and drawn into history without ceasing to be bodies. They do not turn into signs or positions in discourse. Their materiality continues to matter – including their material capacities to engender, to give birth, to give milk, to give and receive pleasure. At the same time, social process must be understood as including such bodily activities as childbirth and infant care, growth and ageing, the pleasures of sexuality and sport, the bodily effort and injury of labour, death from AIDS and equally the struggle to live with AIDS. There is no paradox in the 'social – biological – social' chain of causation identified in Kemper's investigation of testosterone, mentioned earlier in this chapter. This is a typical example of social embodiment.

Social embodiment may involve an individual's conduct, but also may involve a group, an institution, or a whole complex of institutions. For instance, subcultural marking of gender via fetish clothes, in the sexual subcultures mentioned earlier, has meaning only in the life of the group; that is why we speak of a 'leather scene', etc. This is not peculiar to sexual minorities; straight versions of gender are also sustained collectively.

Consider the body-reflexive practice that goes into the exemplary masculinity of a sports star – for instance, the 'iron man' Steve whose situation I describe in *The Men and the Boys* (Connell 2000). The star's practice includes the training routines worked out by coaches, drawing on the professional expertise of physical education and sports medicine. It includes the practice of the sport itself, which is organized by multi-million-dollar corporations (sports associations, franchise businesses). It includes participating in publicity and managing finance via other corporations (commercial media, advertisers). A major sports star, like other media figures, practically turns into a one-person corporation, employing lawyers, accountants, marketing agents, public relations personnel, and others. There is an elaborate social process here. Yet all of this specialized work is based on, and refers back to, the body's physical performances.

Gender always involves social embodiment in this sense. Gender relations form a particular social structure, refer to particular features of bodies, and form a circuit between them.

Gender refers to the bodily structures and processes of human reproduction. These structures and processes do not constitute a 'biological base', a natural mechanism that has social effects. Rather, they constitute an *arena*, a bodily site where something social happens. Among the things that happen is the creation of the cultural categories 'women' and 'men' (and any other gender categories that a particular society marks out). I will call this the *reproductive arena* in social life.

Biological reproduction does not cause gender practice, or even provide a template for it. There are many fields where strongly gendered practice occurs which has not the slightest logical connection with biological reproduction. This becomes abundantly clear in the case of new industries.

Miriam Glucksmann's detailed study of the electrical engineering and food processing industries in inter-war Britain, *Women Assemble* (1990), provides an abundant demonstration. Gender segregation in the new factories, and differential pay between women and men, were introduced on a massive scale. This was neither for biological nor for technical reasons. Nothing about the workers' bodies, nor about the technology of chocolate biscuit production, required segregation, any more than the technology of frying burgers in a contemporary McDonald's fast food outlet requires gender segregation. Segregation was introduced in the biscuit factories for quite a different reason. To have integrated the workplace would have broken down the existing social dependence of women and the gender division of labour at home. Preserving the overall gender division of society mattered more to the men making the decisions, than equity, profit or efficiency.

Social embodiment also applies in cases where the properties of bodies obviously do matter – for instance, gender patterns in health and illness. A body-machine approach would see 'men's health' and 'women's health' as issues constituted by the biological differences of male and female bodies. But that is not the way the women's health movement began. Rather, this movement was concerned from the start with the relation between women's bodies and the gendered structure of health services. Activists criticized the way that the power and ideology of men, especially in medical professions dominated by men, interfered with women getting the health services they needed (Schofield et al. 2000). Some of the health needs of women are different from those of men, some are the same as those of men, but all were affected by the location of women and men in the gender division of labour, and by gender ideologies (for instance, religious ideologies opposed to women having choice about abortion).

Here we have large-scale circuits of body-reflexive practice, involving medical institutions, markets and ideologies. They produce material effects on women's bodies but are also called into play by the material needs of those bodies. The same pattern can be found in 'men's health'. In a recent survey of men's health research in Australia (Connell et al. 1999) one of the strongest gender differences appeared in a study of rural people's eyes. Of the patients with penetrating eye injuries 88 per cent were men. This is not because men's eyes have weaker surfaces than women's. It is because women in rural Australia are rarely given jobs involving hammering on metal or stretching fencing wire, the main sources of this kind of injury. It is the social division of labour that is crucial to understanding these effects – but it is the bodies which bear them.

Bodies are transformed in social embodiment. Some changes are familiar: lengthening expectation of life, as a result of social changes; also rising average height and weight (as nutrition and child health care improve), and changing patterns of disease (e.g. polio declining, TB declining but now reviving).

The transformation of bodies is structured, in part, on gender lines. The demographic indicators themselves show this. In the rich industrial countries women's average life expectancy has now reached 109 per cent of men's. In India, women's average life expectancy is 101 per cent of men's; in Bangladesh and Nepal, men on average outlive women. The gendered industrial economy impacts differently on men's and women's bodies. There are higher rates of industrial and vehicle accidents among men, who are the majority of workers in heavy industry and transport. There are higher rates of repetition strain injury (RSI) among women, who are the majority of keyboard workers.

The idea of social embodiment, involving long circuits of practice, allows us to recognize an important but un-theorized aspect of gender. Many gender processes involve bodily processes and capacities that are *not sex-differentiated*, that are in fact common capacities of women and men.

Among the most important is the bodily capacity to labour. There are almost no sex differences of any consequence in capacities to work, apart from those created by different training, the treatment of pregnancy as a disability, etc. Most production processes in modern industry involve the co-operation of very large numbers of men and women in an intricate flow of work. Ironically, the shared labour of large numbers of men and women creates the material equipment and institutions through which images of gender difference themselves are circulated. The Super Bowl, the faces of Madonna and Mike Tyson, Kylie Minogue and Mel Gibson, go out around the world in their hundreds of millions only because of the shared work of the women and men who build the TV sets, make the paper, and labour for the media corporations which hire the stars and buy the air-time.

As large-scale production assumes, capacities for communication are also shared between men and women. There is a minor industry attempting to define differences between 'women's language' and 'men's language'. An American best-seller assured men that *You Just Don't Understand* what women say, and the author, Deborah Tannen (1990), became a media celebrity.

Most of this is froth. The weakness of the two-cultures approach to language and gender is shown by an excellent critique in the psychologist Mary Crawford's *Talking Difference* (1995). Language use is situational, and is shaped by relations of power. There are no fixed differences between men's and women's language use. As the meta-analyses discussed in the previous section show, there are also no broad gender differences in verbal ability. Specific and situational differences do sometimes appear. But they pale in comparison with the huge overlap in language use between women and men, and the common capacity for language learning. The capacity for language learning is a species characteristic which underpins the whole of culture – including the ideology of gender difference. Strangely, both women and men are able to read and understand the same books about gender difference in language.

Recognizing social embodiment also allows a new view of the relation between bodies and change in gender. In sociobiology, sex role theory, liberal feminism and popular ideologies of natural difference, bodily difference is understood to be a conservative force. It holds back historical change, limits what social process can accomplish, or defines an original state from which society has departed at its peril. By contrast, to radical interpreters of psychoanalysis such as the philosopher Herbert Marcuse (1955), bodily needs could be a subversive force. They could pit the person against social control, or provide energies that might crack open the social order.

Social embodiment indicates a third possibility. Bodies as agents in social practice are involved in the very construction of the social world, the bringing-into-being of social reality. The social world is never simply reproduced. It is always reconstituted by practice.

Gender as a structure of relations is constituted in this historical process, and accordingly can never be fixed, nor exactly reproduced. The strategic question is not 'can gender change?' but 'in what direction is gender changing?' Any situation admits of a range of possible responses.

Even in highly oppressive situations, social groups actually generate a range of responses. For instance, the married women in the cigarette factory studied by Anna Pollert in *Girls, Wives, Factory Lives* (1981) faced a relentless grind at home and at work. From the continuous labour, heavy-handed management, poor wages and broken shifts in the factory they escaped only to a round of cooking, cleaning, childcare and other labour at home. The result was fatigue, strain and depression, according to one respondent: 'Sometimes I think I could throw all this work out of the window. Sometimes it gets on top of you . . . I just feel I want to pack it all in. I want to get miles away. I just can't go on any more. I don't want to go home and start getting the tea, but I do.' The pressure is much the same for all. However the responses of different women ranged widely, from stoic acceptance, through fantasy escape (notably colourful holidays, in the imagination), to resistance by creating a shop-floor culture, to trade union militancy. (At least for a time: their union happened to be controlled by men, and when the women went on strike it let them down.)

The reproductive arena is not fixed, it can be re-shaped by social processes. Indeed it constantly is being reshaped; there is social struggle over this as well as other aspects of gender. For instance, the fertility of a woman's body means something different where contraception is effective and small families are planned, from what it means where women are designated lifelong breeders and nurturers – barefoot, pregnant and in the kitchen, as the saying goes. There is social conflict over the potential meaning of women's fertility. 'Right-to-Life' militants are not just attempting to outlaw abortion: they seek to push the whole reproductive arena into the pattern they call 'the traditional family'. It is no accident that very few Right-to-Life activists campaign for the one straightforward and practical solution to the problem of abortion – effective contraception.

It is possible for social practice to move gender orders in different directions, and create different relations between bodies and social structures. The liberal-feminist idea expressed by Maccoby and Jacklin (quoted above), that a society can choose the gender order it wants, is sociologically naive. A society divided by conflicting interests does not 'choose' as a unit. But Maccoby and Jacklin were not mistaken in seeing a range of historical possibilities in gender relations. There are different futures towards which contemporary societies might be moved, by mobilizing social forces on a sufficiently large scale. I will return to this issue in chapter 8.

4

Gender Relations

Patterns in gender

Chapter 2 included two studies of organizations, Barrie Thorne's study of American elementary schools and Dunbar Moodie's study of South African mines. Each of these organizations had a regular set of arrangements about gender: who was recruited to do what work (most of the teachers were women, all of the mineworkers were men); what social divisions were recognized (e.g. creating 'opposite sides' in the playground); how emotional relations were conducted (e.g. the 'mine wives'); and how these institutions were related to others (e.g. the families of the workers).

Such a pattern in gender arrangements may be called the *gender regime* of an institution. Research on a very wide range of organizations has mapped their gender regimes – schools, offices, factories, armies, police forces, sporting clubs. It is clear that gender regimes are a usual feature of organizational life.

These studies make clear that the gender regime of an institution can change – though change is often resisted. An example is the merger of two gender-segregated English secondary schools described in a very interesting ethnography by Joan Draper (1993). After the merger some boys tried to establish dominance in the new social space, some girls accepted subordination, other girls fought it. Meanwhile other boys began experimenting with gender and turned up in dyed hair, eyeshadow and nail polish. The teachers found the turmoil hard to handle and some became distressed at the loss of their previously established place in the educational world. Over time, however, a new gender regime crystallized.

When Thorne went into Oceanside Elementary School and found that most of the teachers were women, she was not exactly surprised. That is the usual arrangement in elementary schools in the United States. Similarly, Moodie was not astonished to find an all-male workforce at the Witwatersrand gold mines he investigated. That is the usual arrangement in South African mines, and in mining all over the world.

The gender regimes of these particular organizations, then, are part of wider patterns, which also endure over time. As in chapter 1, I call these wider patterns the *gender order* of a society. The gender regimes of institutions usually correspond to the overall gender order, but may depart from it. This is important for change. Some institutions change quickly, others lag; or to put it another way, change often starts in one sector of society and takes time to seep through into other sectors.

When we look at a set of gender arrangements, whether the gender regime of an institution or the gender order of a whole society, we are basically looking at a set of *relationships* – ways that people, groups, and organizations are connected and divided. 'Gender relations' are the relationships arising in and around the reproductive arena discussed in chapter 3. Not all gender relations are direct interactions between women on one side and men on the other. The relations may be indirect – mediated, for instance, by a market, or by technologies such as TV or the Internet. Relationships may be among men, or among women, but still are gender relations – such as hierarchies of masculinity among men.

Gender relations are always being constituted in everyday life. If we don't bring it into being, gender does not exist. This point is forcibly made by ethnomethodology, a school of sociological research concerned with what we presuppose in everyday conduct. Candace West and Don Zimmerman, in a celebrated article called 'Doing Gender' (1987), show an impressive range of ways in which everyday speech constitutes gender relations. Not only are speakers identified in terms of their gender. Relationships between them, such as dominance, deference, antagonism, solidarity, are constantly being enacted in the course of conversations which are nominally about quite different subjects.

Yet we are not free to enact gender however we like. In reality, gender practice is powerfully constrained. When I, as an Australian academic in the 2000s, relate to people in gendered ways, I am not free to use the practices of a slave-owning Athenian aristocrat of the fifth century BC. Wrong meanings would be attached to my actions, and I would doubtless find time to work out my errors in gender theory from a cell in Long Bay Gaol.

Social theory has attempted to capture the fact of constraint and the patterns in relationships with the concept of *structure*. Relations among people (or among groups or institutions) would have little significance if they were randomly arranged. Patterns in these relations would matter little if they were ephemeral. It is the enduring or extensive patterns among social relations that social theory calls 'structures'.

The gender arrangements of a society involve social structure in this sense. For instance, if religious, political and conversational practices all place men in authority over women, we speak of a patriarchal structure of gender relations. Or if clans of men regularly marry each others' sisters, we speak of a kinship structure of exchange.

A structure of relations does not mechanically determine how people or groups act. That was the error of deterministic marxism. But a structure of relations certainly defines possibilities and consequences. For instance, the structure of gender relations in Australian society did not fix what sexual practices Huey Brown (chapter 2) would engage in. But they gave him a definite set of possibilities. When he took up certain of them – continuing sex with men, drag, and domestic partnership – the structure of gender relations defined powerful consequences for his life, which are traced in Gary Dowsett's case study.

In this sense, social structure conditions practice. This does not imply that structures cause, or exist separately from, practices. The structure of gender relations has no existence outside the practices through which people and groups conduct those relations. Structures do not continue, cannot be 'enduring', unless they are reconstituted from moment to moment in social action. In this sense gender, even in its most elaborate, abstract or fantastic forms, is always an 'accomplishment', as West and Zimmerman have put it. Gender is something actually done; and done in social life, not something that exists prior to social life.

Four dimensions of gender

When the pioneering British feminist Juliet Mitchell published *Woman's Estate* in 1971, she argued that women's oppression involves not one, but four structures: production, reproduction, socialization and sexuality.

Why make such distinctions? Many discussions of gender do not. For instance, the feminist lawyer Catharine MacKinnon (1989), developing a theory of the state and the gender dimension of law, treats 'gender hierarchy' as a homogeneous whole. The anthropologist Gayle Rubin (1975), in a very influential model of the 'sex/gender system', treated the whole field as a single system. But when we look closely into these theories, it becomes clear that each prioritizes a particular kind of relationship (MacKinnon: domination; Rubin: kinship). If we were to put power relations and kinship together in a more comprehensive picture of gender, we would need at least a two-dimensional model.

There are also practical reasons for acknowledging multiple dimensions in gender relations. We often experience disparities in gender relations, as if part of our lives were working on one gender logic, and another part on a different logic. When this happens in public life, not just in personal affairs, the complexity within the gender system becomes highly visible.

For instance, the modern liberal state defines men and women as citizens, that is, as alike. But the dominant sexual code defines men and women as opposites. Meanwhile customary ideas about the division of labour in family life define women as housewives and carers of children. Accordingly women entering the public domain – trying to exercise their rights as citizens – have an uphill battle to have their authority recognized. They may try to solve this problem by becoming 'honorary men', tougher than the toughest, like Margaret Thatcher in Britain and Madeleine Albright in the United States. But most women in politics, like Hillary Clinton in the United States and Cheryl Kernot in Australia, have to struggle for credibility.

The political scientist Carole Pateman (1988) dramatized this disparity in her argument that the 'social contract' of liberal society was underpinned by a 'sexual contract', the private subordination of women to men. This gave the whole of liberal democracy the character of a 'fraternal social contract', an agreement among men. The statistics of political participation given in chapter 1 suggest this is still broadly true, around the world.

At times such disparities become so striking that they stimulate a strong cultural response. The sixteenth-century cult of 'Gloriana' is a fascinating example. Elizabeth Tudor became queen of England under rules of inheritance that preferred men but admitted women as residual heirs. She became a skilful politician, riding out rebellion and financial crisis, successfully managing deep religious tensions and the changing social forces represented in parliament – which broke out into revolution a few decades after her death. She was, in the language of the day, a strong monarch. But her authority was in flagrant contradiction with the ideas of a patriarchal society. To maintain legitimacy she and her supporters had to construct a new sexual identity (stalling endlessly on marriage negotiations, and celebrating the 'Virgin Queen') and a mixed-gender position as leader of a new cult of nationality. In a famous speech she gave at the time of the invasion threat from the Spanish Armada, Elizabeth put it this way:

> I know I have the body of a weak and feeble woman, but I have the heart and stomach of a king, and of a king of England too, and think foul scorn that [the duke of] Parma or [the king of] Spain, or any prince of Europe should dare to invade the borders of my realm; to which, rather than any dishonour shall grow by me, I myself will take up arms, I myself will be your general, judge, and rewarder of every one of your virtues in the field. (Neale 1960: 302)

An extraordinary literary cult was fostered, which by late in her reign was almost defining her as a supernatural being. This genre includes Spenser's *The Faerie Queene*, one of the great English epic poems.

There is, then, a strong case for seeing gender relations as internally complex, as involving multiple structures. If that general case is accepted, how are we to identify and map the structures involved?

Mitchell's original model mainly distinguished types of practice – work, child-rearing and sexuality – but also mixed these with social functions, such as 'reproduction' and 'socialization'. Apart from some logical inconsistency, this approach has limitations. It is clear, for instance, that rather different gender relations can exist in the same kind of practice. Consider, for instance, the range of social relations involved in 'sexuality', as shown in Dowsett's study of Harriet Brown.

An alternative approach is to identify different social dynamics, or processes of change, and try to work back to their internal logic. This was the approach taken by classical socialism, which identified the dynamic of class struggle and worked back to a structural analysis of capitalism. It is the approach of single-structure theories of patriarchy, which starts with the political dynamic of feminism and describes the system of power and oppression that feminism confronts.

A sophisticated development of this idea was offered by Sylvia Walby in *Theorizing Patriarchy* (1990), which distinguishes six structures in contemporary patriarchy: paid employment, household production, culture, sexuality, violence, and the state. This greatly improves the kind of model seen in MacKinnon's work. Walby's model is still a model of patriarchy, that is to say, institutionalized inequality in gender relations. If we want to include in the picture of gender patterns that are not inherently unequal, we need a different formulation.

The model I suggest is a development from the one that I proposed in *Gender and Power* (Connell 1987). It distinguishes four dimensions of gender, describing four main structures in the modern system of gender relations. Later in the chapter I will discuss how these structures change. Here I will outline them and comment on their significance.

Power relations

Power, as a dimension of gender, was central to the Women's Liberation concept of 'patriarchy', and to the social analyses that flowed from it: the idea of men as a dominant 'sex class', the analysis of rape as an assertion of men's power over women, and the critique of media images of women as passive, trivial and dumb.

Women's Liberation recognized that patriarchal power was not just a matter of direct control of women by individual men, but was also realized impersonally through the state. A classic example, analysed in a famous article by Catharine MacKinnon (1983), is court procedure in rape cases. Independent of any personal bias of the judge, the procedures by which rape charges are tried effectively place the complainant rather than the defendant 'on trial'. The woman's sexual history, marital situation and motives in laying a charge are all under scrutiny.

Many attempts at legal reform have been made since, and have proved that the inbuilt biases in social assumptions and court procedure about sexual assault are very difficult to eliminate. It can still be a damaging experience for a woman to bring charges. A very public example of the difficulty occurred in Sydney in late 2000. A young woman made a complaint to police about an event during a party in the Parliament buildings, involving a sexual approach by a Member of Parliament in his office (he said the approach was consensual, she said it was not). The Speaker of the House (a man who belonged to the same party as the MP in question) responded by collecting derogatory evidence from an aide about the *woman's* behaviour on the night in question. The woman dropped the complaint, to avoid the impact of publicity on her private life. Nevertheless an official inquiry was held in a blaze of publicity, into the possibility of corrupt conduct by the Speaker, his aide and the MP. All were cleared.

Another important case of the institutionalization of power relations is bureaucracies. Clare Burton, an Australian social scientist who also served in public life as an equal opportunity commissioner, spoke of the 'mobilization of masculine bias' in selection and promotion of staff. By this she meant the impersonal but pervasive tendency, in organizations dominated by men, to favour criteria and procedures that favour men (Burton 1987).

Power also emerged as a major theme in Gay Liberation writing such as Dennis Altman's *Homosexual: Oppression and Liberation* (1972). In this case the focus was on power applied to a specific group of men: criminalization, police harassment, economic discrimination, and violence. Gay Liberation theorists linked the oppression of gay men with the oppression of lesbians and the oppression of women generally. This argument laid the foundation for the analysis of gendered power relations among men, and the distinction of hegemonic from subordinated masculinities (Carrigan, Connell and Lee 1985) which is important in current research on men and masculinities.

Power operating through institutions, power in the form of oppression of one group by another, is an important part of the structure of gender. But there is another approach to power, popularized by the French historian and philosopher Michel Foucault (1977). Foucault was sceptical of the idea that there was a unified, central agency of power in society. Rather, he argued, power is widely dispersed, and operates intimately and diffusely. Especially it operates discursively, through the ways we talk, write and conceptualize. This diffuse but tenacious power operates close up, not at a distance. It impacts directly on people's bodies as 'discipline' as well as on their identities and sense of their place in the world.

This post-structuralist approach appealed to many feminist as well as gay theorists, who saw here a way of understanding the fine texture, as well as the strength, of gendered power. Power is present intimately. The discourse of fashion and beauty, for instance, positions women as consumers, subjects them to humiliating tests of acceptability, enforces arbitrary rules and is responsible for much unhappiness, ill health, and even some deaths (among young women whose dieting goes out of control). Yet there is no Patriarchy Central compelling women to do all this. As the 'lip gloss' in Barrie Thorne's ethnography illustrates, girls and young women enter the world of fashion and beauty because they want to, because it delivers pleasures, and because the regulation and discipline are bound up with the identity they are seeking.

Both these approaches to power contribute to our understanding of gender relations: they are not exclusive. There is both organized, institutional power and diffuse, discursive power. And both approaches raise the crucial question of resistance.

To give a full account of power relations requires an account of the way power is contested, and countervailing power is mobilized. Total domination is extremely rare; even fascist dictatorships could not accomplish that. Gendered power is no more total than other kinds.

Oppressive laws are met by campaigns for reform – such as the most famous of all feminist campaigns, the 'suffragette' struggle for the vote. Domestic patriarchy may be weakened, or manoeuvred around, by the inhabitants of the 'red chamber' (as the classic Chinese novel put it), the women of the household.

Discursive power can also be contested or transformed. The remarkable work of the Australian educator Bronwyn Davies shows that challenges to patriarchy need not involve head-on confrontation. In *Shards of Glass* (1993) Davies shows how educators in the classroom can help children and youth gain control of gender discourses. Young people can learn how they are discursively positioned and regulated, and can learn to shift between, or manoeuvre among, identities.

The conditions for resistance change in history. The modern liberal state, which emerged in Europe and North America in the eighteenth and nineteenth centuries, creates possibilities for mass politics which did not exist before. Monarchical states and household patriarchies did not depend on notions of citizenship; the liberal state does. In that sense, the development of patriarchal institutions themselves created the conditions for the emergence of modern feminism.

Production relations

The 'sexual division of labour' was the first structure of gender to be recognized in social science, and remains the centre of most discussions of gender in anthropology and economics. In many societies, and in many situations, certain tasks are performed by men and others are performed by women. So, in the Aboriginal communities of the Australian central desert, hunting wallabies and kangaroos was undertaken by men, collecting root vegetables and seeds was mainly undertaken by women. In contemporary North America teaching young children is mainly done by women; in South Africa underground mining is entirely done by men.

Such divisions of labour are common throughout history and across cultures. But while gender divisions of labour are extremely common, there is not exactly the same division in different cultures or at different points of history. The same task may be 'women's work' in one context, and 'men's work' in another. Agricultural labour – digging and planting – is an important example.

A striking modern case is secretarial work. Being a clerk was originally a man's job – as described in Herman Melville's dark short story 'Bartleby the Scrivener' (1853). With the advent of the typewriter and the growing scale of office work, clerical work increasingly involved women; in fact it became archetypical 'women's work', as Rosemary Pringle shows in *Secretaries Talk* (1989). But with the advent of the computer and word processing, 'the secretary' is disappearing as an occupational category. Clerical work is again, increasingly, being done by men.

In modern Western society, gender divisions between jobs are not the whole of the gender division of labour. There is a larger division between 'work' – the realm of paid labour and production for markets – and 'home'. The whole economic sphere is culturally defined as men's world (regardless of the presence of women in it), while domestic life is defined as women's world (regardless of the presence of men in it).

The Norwegian sociologist Øystein Holter (1995, 1997) argues that this division is the structural basis of the modern Western gender order. It is what makes this system different from the gender orders of non-Western, non-capitalist societies. His point is not only that our notions of 'masculinity' and 'femininity' are closely connected with this division. Just as important, the social relations that govern work in these two spheres are different. In the economy, work is done for pay, labour is bought and sold, and the products of labour are placed on a market where profit prevails. In the home, work is done for love (or from mutual obligation), the products of labour are a gift, the logic of gift-exchange prevails. From these structural differences, Holter argues, flow characteristically different experiences for men and women – and our ideas about the different natures of men and women.

This is not exactly a distinction between 'production' and 'consumption', though that has been suggested by others as the economic core of the gender system. Domestic 'consumption' requires work, just as much as factory-based 'production'. Housewives do not spend their time lolling on couches and scoffing chocolates. Housework and childcare are hard work and the hours have remained long, despite the advent of 'labour-saving' machines like vacuum cleaners and microwave ovens. But housework and job-work are done in different social relations, as Holter correctly observes, and they consequently have very different cultural meanings.

The division of labour itself is only part of a larger process. In a modern economy the shared work of women and men is embodied in every major product, and every major service – therefore in the process of economic growth. Yet women and men are differently located in that process, and as the statistics of income in chapter 1 show, women and men get different benefits from it.

What can be seen here is a *gendered accumulation process*. Maria Mies (1986), the German socialist feminist who has formulated this issue most clearly, suggests that the global economy has developed through a dual process of colonization and 'housewifization'. Women in the colonized world, formerly full participants in local non-capitalist economies, have been increasingly pressed into the 'housewife' pattern of social isolation and dependence on a male breadwinner.

Accumulation in modern economies is organized through large corporations and global markets. The gender regimes of these institutions make it possible for them to apply the products of men's and women's joint work in gendered ways. The way firms distribute corporate income – through wage structures, benefits packages, etc. – tends to favour men, especially middle-class men. The products that corporations place on the market have gender effects and gendered uses, from cosmetics to armaments.

The gendered accumulation process has many effects beyond the 'economy' narrowly defined. For instance, where there is a gender division of labour in occupations – such as men being the majority in engineering and mechanical trades, women in arts-based and human service jobs – there will be a division in the education systems which prepare people for this work. It is not surprising to find that enrolments in school courses in 'engineering studies' and 'computer sciences' are overwhelmingly boys, while enrolments in 'fine arts' and 'hospitality' are mainly girls.

Emotional relations

The importance of emotional attachment in human life was made clear a hundred years ago by Sigmund Freud (1900). Borrowing ideas from neurology but mainly learning from his own case studies, Freud showed how charges of emotion – both positive and negative – were attached, in the unconscious mind, to images of other people. His famous analysis of the 'oedipus complex', the centrepiece of his theory of personality development, showed how important the patterning of these attachments, or cathexes, might be. (For clear and careful definitions of these terms see *The Language of Psycho-Analysis*: Laplanche and Pontalis 1973.)

In fact Freud was speaking not only about the individual mind, but also about the pattern of relationships inside an important social institution, the bourgeois family. He thus opened up for investigation the structure of emotional relations, attachments or commitments. This is an important dimension of gender, often interwoven with power and the division of labour (e.g. in the figures of the father and the mother), but also following its own logic.

Emotional commitments may be positive or negative, favourable or hostile towards the object. For instance, prejudice against women (misogyny), or against homosexuals (homophobia), is a definite emotional relationship. Emotional commitments may also be, as Freud emphasized, both loving and hostile at once. Ambivalence, as this state is called, is common in reality though it tends to be forgotten in gender myths and stereotypes.

A major arena of emotional attachment is sexuality. Anthropological and historical studies have made it clear that sexual relations involve culturally formed bodily relationships, not a simple biological reflex (Caplan 1987). They have a definable social structure. The main axis on which contemporary Western sexuality is organized is gender: the division between cross-gender (heterosexual) and same-gender (homosexual) relations. This distinction is so important that we treat it as defining different kinds of people ('homosexuals', 'heterosexuals'), and certain biologists go looking for a 'homosexual gene' to explain the difference. (However, no one has gone looking for the 'heterosexual gene'.)

But cross-cultural research shows that many societies do not make this distinction. They have both same-gender and cross-gender sexual encounters, but they do not arrange them the way we do, nor think they define different types of people. For instance, the 'Sambia', a community in Papua New Guinea described in a well-known ethnography by Gilbert Herdt, *Guardians of the Flutes* (1981), treat same-gender sexuality as a ritual practice that all men are involved in at a particular stage of life. From a Western point of view, all Sambia men are homosexuals at one age, and all switch over to become heterosexuals at another. That is absurd, of course. From a Sambia point of view, they are simply following the normal development of masculinity.

In contemporary Western society, households are expected to be formed on the basis of romantic love, that is, a strong individual attachment between two partners. This ideal is promoted in mass media and popular fiction, and its importance is confirmed by research with groups who might be thought sceptical of it. They include the men in Gary Dowsett's study (Harriet Brown was not alone wanting to live in a loving couple); and the American college students in an ethnography by Dorothy Holland and Margaret Eisenhart, *Educated in Romance* (1990).

Where this pattern holds, sexual attachment is now the main basis of household formation. The cultural dominance of the West has meant a shift, in many post-colonial situations, from the choice of a marriage partner by one's parents to the choice of a partner by personal attraction – romantic love. The resulting tensions are explored in the recent comedy *East is East*, a film about an Anglo-Pakistani family struggling about arranged marriages, Muslim tradition, and British working-class realities. Curmudgeonly conservatives warned that the shift from marriages arranged by wise parents to marriages contracted by impetuous youth risked the collapse of a household when the sexual interest died. The historically startling level of divorce in the United States – where according to very recent sample survey data, 43 per cent of first marriages end in separation or divorce within fifteen years – shows they were right.

Emotional relations are also found in the workplace (and not just in the form of office sex). Rosemary Pringle's study, already mentioned, shows how emotional relations with bosses help to construct the very job of 'secretary'. Arlie Hochschild's classic *The Managed Heart* (1983) analyses emotional labour in the modern economy. There are many jobs where producing a particular emotional relationship with a customer is central to the work being done. These are, typically, gender-typed jobs. Hochschild's main examples are airline hostesses, a job where workers are trained to produce sympathy and induce relaxation; and telephone debt collectors, a job where workers must display aggression and induce fear. Hochschild argues that this kind of labour is becoming more common with the expansion of service industries. If so, alienated relations based on commercialized feelings and gender stereotypes may be increasingly important in modern life.

Hostile emotional relationships are not only symbolic, like the ones enacted by Hochschild's debt collectors. They may involve all too real practices of oppression. Stephen Tomsen's (1998) study of homophobic killings, for instance, shows two major patterns of conduct. One is gang attacks in public places by young men who go looking for gender deviants to punish, a process that depends on mutual encouragement in the group. The other is killings by individuals in private. Some of these involve a violent response to a sexual approach (and perhaps to the killers' own desires) which they think calls their masculinity into question. Both patterns may result in killings of extreme brutality.

Emotional relations go beyond the face-to-face. Nationalism, as Joane Nagel (1998) points out, constantly uses gender imagery in constructing national solidarities. We are all familiar with the 'family of the nation', the 'father of his country', the heroic soldier dying to protect his womenfolk, 'Mother Russia', the nation as goddess. It is no accident that, as

Irina Novikova (chapter 2 above) and Svetlana Slapšak (2000) show, new nationalisms in the former communist countries of eastern Europe are reasserting highly traditional gender images.

Symbolic relations

All social practice involves interpreting the world. As post-structuralists observe, nothing human is 'outside' discourse. Society is unavoidably a world of meanings. At the same time, meanings bear the traces of the social processes by which they were made. This is the fundamental point made by the sociology of knowledge. Cultural systems bear particular social interests, and grow out of historically specific ways of life.

This point applies to gender meanings. Whenever we speak of 'a woman' or 'a man', we call into play a tremendous system of understandings, implications, overtones and allusions that have accumulated through our cultural history. The 'meanings' of these words are enormously greater than the biological categories of male and female. When the Papua New Guinea highland community studied by Marilyn Strathern (1978) say 'our clan is a clan of men', they do not mean that the clan entirely consists of males. When an American football coach yells at his losing team that they are 'a bunch of women', he does not mean they can now get pregnant. But both are saying something meaningful, and in their contexts, important.

The best-known model of the structure of symbolism in gender derives from the French psychoanalyst Jacques Lacan. Lacan's analysis of the phallus as master-symbol gave rise to an interpretation of language as 'phallocentric', a system in which the place of authority, the privileged subjectivity, is always that of the masculine. The potentially infinite play of meaning in language is fixed by the phallic point of reference; culture itself embodies the 'law of the father'. If that is so, the only way to contest patriarchal meanings is to escape known forms of language. Hence feminist thinkers in the 1970s, such as Xavière Gauthier, developed an interest in women's writing as an oppositional practice that had to subvert the laws of culture. (For translations of Gauthier, and other French feminists on this question, see Marks and de Courtivron 1981.)

Chris Weedon (1987) wonders how feminist theory could have adopted so deterministic a psychology, which gives no room for opposition, only for escape. There are certainly other schools of psychoanalysis which offer more open-ended accounts of gender and suggest more possibilities for action. Nevertheless the dichotomous gender structuring of culture is important, and the Lacanian approach gives us some inkling of why patriarchal gender arrangements are so difficult to abolish. To do so involves uprooting, not just a few intolerant attitudes, but a whole system of communication and meaning. Queen Elizabeth, addressing her men at Tilbury, acknowledged 'the body of a weak and feeble woman', but claimed 'the heart and stomach of a king'. She could not have reversed her symbolism, and claimed 'the heart and stomach of a woman', if she were to motivate her troops to fight.

Though language – speech and writing – is the most analysed site of symbolic gender relations, it is not the only one. Gender symbolism also operates in dress, makeup, gesture, in photography and film, and in more impersonal forms of culture such as the built environment.

Elizabeth Wilson's (1987) elegant study of fashion, *Adorned in Dreams,* shows that women's and men's styles of dress not only symbolize gender difference, but are also a site of struggle over what women and men are allowed to do. The famous 'bloomers' of nineteenth-century dress reform were connected with the struggle to expand the rights of women. For a short while bloomers were adopted by suffrage activists. They were jeered at by conservatives because they symbolized emancipated women (not that they changed women's activities in practice). Similarly in the 1960s the new fashion styles were connected with young women's demand for sexual freedom, and were duly denounced as licentious. Jean Shrimpton, a visiting British fashion model, created a media scandal in Australia by going to the Melbourne Cup races in a mini-dress and – an unforgivable offence – without gloves!

Rosa Linda Fregoso's *The Bronze Screen* (1993) illustrates the play of gender relations in film – in this case, films produced by Chicana/ Chicano film-makers, about the community of Mexican affiliation in the south-western USA. Chicano (men) film-makers, Fregoso observes, have not demeaned their women characters, but they have not given them an active role in discourse. Only with the advent of woman film-makers did films start to explore generational difference, language, religion and relationships from women's standpoints, and show some of the tensions and ambiguities in women's position and responses. Architectural design also reflects assumptions about gender dichotomy and gendered spaces, and grows out of the designers' gendered experience. Annmarie Adams and Peta Tancred in *Designing Women* (2000), a study of gender and architecture in Canada, found that the imagery in professional journals persistently associated women with interiors, especially domestic interiors, but presented architects as 'powerful, virile, and masculine'. However, this pattern of marginalization changed as women arrived in the profession, and became influential in establishing the modernist style.

Symbolic relations in gender include the rules for 'gender attribution' studied by ethnomethodologists. Here we move below the level at which gender categories ordinarily appear, to consider how a person (or action) gets assigned to a gender category. These rules are normally taken for granted in everyday life. But they are painstakingly studied by cross-dressers and transsexuals hoping to 'pass', which requires one to produce an effect of naturalness by deliberate action. Accordingly, transsexuals have appeared to psychiatrists and ethnomethodologists as a kind of natural experiment exposing the cultural underpinnings of the gender system (Kessler and McKenna 1978).

But things get complicated when the transsexuals read the psychiatrists' and ethnomethodologists' books – as some now do. As a warning against over-simplified views of gender, transsexualism itself has now become a gender category, and to a certain extent a sexual subculture. You can buy the international *Tranny Guide* (Vicky Lee 1999) to learn how to do it (with serious advice on body care, how to present at the job, etc.) and how to get in touch with the cross-dressing scene around the world. You can even check this scene out on the Internet (try www.wayout-publishing.com). In a recent book Viviane Namaste (2000) urges attention to the real-life situations and experiences of transsexual and transgendered people – which tend to be 'erased' by queer theory, social science and medicine alike.

The tranny scene is determinedly upbeat, but there is a dark side to violating the cultural categories. Transgender people often face ostracism, loss of jobs, and family hostility, as well as major difficulties in sexual relations. Some have to support themselves by sex work such as stripping and prostitution. As Harriet found, there is a certain clientele of 'straight' men who are excited by transsexuals. But this does not mean they respect them. Roberta Perkins's pioneering book presenting the voices of transsexuals in Sydney includes Naomi, a stripper who remarked:

> I think men have a definite dislike for women in general, that's why women are raped and bashed, and strippers are up there to provide an outlet for this dislike by the yelling of profanities at them. Transsexuals are lower down than women according to men, and look how many men sexually abuse transsexuals. (1983: 73)

Naomi's point about abusive men relates not only to the cultural relations of gender but also to power relations, in the form of sexual violence. She also implies something about production relations –

straight men have the economic resources to be the clients of these services. And of course her remarks relate to emotional relations, in terms of sexual desire and hatred. So all four structures of gender are present in this one situation.

This is usual. In distinguishing four structures of gender relations, I do not mean to suggest they operate in separate compartments of life. They are constantly intermingled and interacting in practice. I distinguish structures *analytically* because tracing out their logic helps in understanding an extremely complex reality. This does not imply that reality itself comes in boxes. Naomi, for one, knows that.

Gender as history

Ideologies of 'natural difference' have drawn much of their force from the traditional belief that gender never changes. Adam delved and Eve span, Men must work and Women must weep, Boys will be Boys. Serious analysis begins with the recognition that exactly the opposite is true: *everything about gender is historical.*

What does 'historical' mean? In the whole story of life on earth, human history represents a new process of change. Some time in the last half-million years, social dynamics replaced organic evolution as the central mechanism of change in our biosphere. Sociobiologists and evolutionary psychologists are not absurd in asking how human society is related to the evolution of the natural world. The same question was the centre of nineteenth-century sociology, when books with titles like *Social Evolution* (Kidd 1898) were best-sellers. But these authors, over-anxious to prove the continuity of evolution, miss the deep change in the process of change. A radically new dynamic was introduced when the collective capacities of humans could be mobilized by social relations. This is why human society, and not organic evolution, can produce cloth, pottery, ziggurats, irrigated rice-fields, rock music and gravity-wave detectors.

Some biological features of human ancestors were certainly preconditions of this change. The open architecture (to borrow a computer term) of the human hand, brain, and speech apparatus makes an immense range of applications possible. The human body, equipped with arm and hand, cannot scratch as sharply as a cat, dig as well as a wombat, swim as fast as a seal, manipulate as delicately as a monkey, or crush as powerfully as a bear. But it can do all those things moderately well; and it can make tools to do them all *very* well. This multiplies the capacities of any one person. Yet the greatest human invention of all is other human beings. We not only create social relations, we teach new generations to operate in, and build on, the social relations already existing. With cumulating effects over time, social relations multiply the capacities of any individual body on the astonishing scale we see all around us. So great a multiplication, ironically, that it now threatens human life by nuclear war or environmental disaster.

The horizon in time where history appears is also the horizon of gender. In the broadest perspective, gender represents the transformation of the system of sexual reproduction by social action. Human collective capacities, organized through social relations, lead to entirely new possibilities. Some are for creativity and pleasure. For instance, sexuality is constructed in culture, and the world of love and eroticism becomes possible. Some are for subjection and exploitation. Patriarchy becomes possible, along with family property, bride-price, convents and prostitution.

Above this horizon is the history of gender: the course of events that has produced the actual gender orders we live in. The history of gender includes the history of practices, and transformations of the body in practice. It includes the production and transformation of the categories of gender. We know these are not fixed; new categories ('the homosexual', 'the housewife') appear and others decline. The history of gender includes the gender regimes of institutions and the gender orders of societies.

This is, in principle, a world history. That idea was first formulated in the nineteenth century, in debates about 'origins' which invented the idea of a primitive matriarchy. The search for origins was resumed in the 1970s in the debate about patriarchy unleashed by Women's Liberation. The search is futile. As the French feminist Christine Delphy (1984) showed in a brilliant critique, origins stories are not history but are a form of myth-making. They create myths in which later social arrangements are explained (and often justified) by a mechanism 'discovered' at the point of origin.

A real history of gender begins with the recognition that the later course of events is *not* contained in any founding moment.

Rather, an open-ended social process is involved, which must be studied in all its complexity by patient examination of the historical records: the archaeological deposits, the written sources, the oral traditions. Local history of this kind has flourished for several decades, being one of the main branches of Women's Studies. It has produced superb work, such as *Family Fortunes* by Leonore Davidoff and Catherine Hall (1987), a social history of gender in the English middle class of the industrial revolution. A world history of gender has taken longer to develop, but now seems to be emerging from two starting points. One is the archaeological reconstruction of gender relations in prehistory and ancient urban cultures (Gero and Conkey 1991). The other is the study of gender relations in modern imperialism, the global process which has at last reversed the proliferation of cultures and begun to create a single world society.

Recognizing the deeply historical character of gender has an important intellectual and political consequence. If a structure can come into existence, it can also go out of existence. The history of gender may have an end.

There are several ways in which gender relations might cease to be important conditions of social life. They might be weakened by an internal uncoupling, so that gender patterns in one domain of practice cease to reinforce those in another. Alternatively, gender relations might be overwhelmed by some other historical dynamic. This was expected by marxists like Alexandra Kollontai, who thought that proletarianization and socialist revolution would end the oppression of women. In our day, the total triumph of the market might do the job.

Finally, gender relations might be extinguished by a deliberate de-gendering, in which the reach of gender structure is reduced to zero. A de-gendering logic is found in some current feminist strategies, such as equal opportunity and anti-discrimination policies. Not all feminists agree with the de-gendering approach, and not all theorists assume a complete de-gendering of society is possible. Even if it is impractical, however, a gender-free society remains an important conceptual benchmark for thinking about change.

The process of change

Most discussions of why gender arrangements change have focused on external pressures on the gender order: changing technology, urban life, the demands of capitalism, mass communications, secularism, modernization or Westernization.

It is true that these social forces can produce change in gender relations. But gender relations also have internal tendencies towards change. Further, some of the 'external' forces are gendered from the start (for instance, the capitalist economic system). In this discussion I will focus on the dynamics of change that arise within gender relations.

Post-structuralist theory has recognized internal tendencies towards change by arguing that gender categories are inherently unstable. For instance, the uncertain and contested character of the category 'women' is a theme of Judith Butler's well-known book *Gender Trouble* (1990). Gender identities are produced discursively. But meanings in discourse are not fixed. Indeed they are inherently unstable, incapable of being fixed.

Further, there is no fixed connection between discursive identities and the bodies to which those identities refer. The signifier is able to float free, in a play of meanings and pleasures. That is sometimes thought to be a general feature of 'postmodern' life, and it certainly suggests that gender identities can be played with, taken up and abandoned, unpacked and recombined. This has been a theme in the 'queer theory' of the 1990s and in other applications of post-structuralist and postmodern ideas.

There are several difficulties with a concept of generalized instability. It can be made true by definition, but in that case is not interesting. If it is open to empirical checking, then it is difficult to avoid the fact that in some historical situations gender identities and relations change slowly, in other situations they change explosively. A good example is Irina Novikova's account of the Soviet and post-Soviet gender orders (chapter 2 above). Nor does a concept of generalized instability give any grip on why some people would want to change gender arrangements, while others would resist changes. This is a question of central importance for the politics of gender. It raises the issue of the differing material interests that different groups have in an unequal society – a question hard to formulate in a purely discursive theory.

The post-structuralist approach is helpful in emphasizing that identities are always historically constructed and in principle open to change; but we need a more specific theory to understand how change occurs. The key is to recognize that structures develop *crisis tendencies*, that is, internal contradictions or tendencies that undermine current patterns and force change in the structure itself.

This approach to change – which draws from German critical theory, especially Jürgen Habermas (1976) – allows us to distinguish periods when pressures for change are well controlled, or are gradually building, from periods when crisis tendencies erupt into actual crisis and force rapid change. It also allows us to identify interests that can be mobilized for and against change, by examining where different groups are located in the structure under pressure, and how they have come into being within that structure. Crisis tendencies can be identified in each of the four structures of gender relations identified earlier in this chapter.

Power relations show the most spectacular recent change. A global movement for the emancipation of women has appeared, challenging men's control of institutions as well as men's power in the intimate spheres of sexuality and the family.

The main crisis tendency here has often been noticed. There is an underlying contradiction between the subordination of women to men in patriarchal homes and workplaces, and the abstract equality between women and men which is presupposed by citizenship and markets. Over the last two centuries this contradiction has sharpened, as the liberal state has developed, and market relations have come to dominate the economy.

Women are the main group subordinated in patriarchal power structures and so have a structural interest in change. Feminist movements, mobilizing women, have been energized by this contradiction and have used it to break down inequality. They have persistently claimed 'rights' in the public sphere and used those rights to challenge oppression in private spheres. The campaign against domestic violence is a notable example (see Rebecca Dobash and Russell Dobash 1992). This campaign, claiming human rights to safety and freedom from fear, has used the patriarchal state itself to enforce these rights when violated by husbands and de factos.

Production relations have also been the site of massive change. Through the second half of the twentieth century there was a worldwide incorporation of women's labour into the market economy. In the industrialized countries this took the form of a huge growth in married women's 'workforce participation' rates, especially in the service sector. In the developing world it took the form of an even more massive move into cities and into market-based agriculture. By the end of the century adult women's workforce participation was over 90 per cent of the men's rate in Cambodia, Ghana, Tanzania, Vietnam, Malawi, Rwanda, Mozambique, Burundi, Guinea, Benin and Sweden – and not far behind that in other parts of Scandinavia, eastern Europe, the former Soviet Union, China, central and west Africa.

There is an underlying contradiction between the equal contribution to social labour by women and men (bearing in mind unpaid as well as paid work) and the gendered appropriation of the products of social labour. The gendered appropriation is seen in the unequal incomes of women and men as groups, the better conditions and career prospects men generally have, and the patriarchal inheritance of wealth. (It is still the general rule in big business that sons may take over the company but daughters hardly ever do.)

Women have a general interest in changing this. One consequence is that women workers make up a growing proportion of union members, and union militants. The story of women's struggle to establish their presence in the union movement is told in Suzanne Franzway's *Sexual Politics and Greedy Institutions* (forthcoming). It is significant that the latest two presidents of the Australian Council of Trade Unions (the unions' peak organization in that country) have been women. But the turbulence of the gendered accumulation process, and its interplay with class and colonial relations, create complex economic situations. An important consequence is that some women – and often the most influential – have an interest in resisting economic reform, because this would disturb the corporate system from which they benefit.

Emotional relations have also seen important recent changes in the industrialized countries. Though lesbians and gay men are still subject to homophobic abuse and violence, homosexual sexuality has to a certain extent achieved legitimacy as an alternative within the heterosexual order. Visible gay and lesbian communities now exist in many cities, anti-discrimination and anti-defamation laws exist in a number of countries, and there is a limited representation of gay and lesbian communities in some political systems and in some areas of policymaking (e.g. in relation to the HIV/AIDS epidemic). As Dennis Altman (1982) pointed out, gay and lesbian communities have achieved a position in some ways resembling that of ethnic minorities.

This is a partial resolution of a long-standing contradiction. The patriarchal gender order prohibits some forms of emotional attachment and pleasure which its own gender arrangements (e.g. homo-social institutions, the oedipal family) produce. A related logic operates within heterosexual relations. The constantly growing incitement to sexual activity (what conservatives call 'permissiveness') contradicts the continuing definition of women as sexually passive, as the objects of men's desire and seduction. The result has been an uneven pattern of change, seen in surveys of sexual behaviour, where women's sexual repertoire has been growing but the 'double standard' for women and men remains.

Symbolic relations are the home ground of generalized-instability arguments, which centre on the discursive construction of identities. It might therefore seem difficult to define crisis tendencies here. But what has made it possible to recognize unstable identities is a tendency towards crisis in the legitimation of patriarchy.

Patriarchy has long been legitimated by belief systems which picture gender as a timeless, unchanging division – whether laid down by God or fixed by the genes – which makes 'woman's place' the right place for ever and ever. Over the last century and a half, social and intellectual movements have chipped away at these assumptions: from the woman suffrage movement and psychoanalysis to Gay Liberation and post-structuralism. Natural-difference ideas remain very influential in popular culture. But over time their capacity to form the unquestioned common sense of society has been undermined. In an era when 'sex changes' are reported in the media, governments have Equal Opportunity targets, and global conferences on gender reform occur, it is difficult to take for granted a timeless male/female opposition.

A vast change in presuppositions has thus occurred in the cultural life of the industrial (and many industrializing) countries. A hundred years ago those who claimed equality for women, or rights for homosexuals, had to justify the claim against presuppositions to the contrary. Now those who deny equality or rights have to justify their denial against a presumption for equality and a presumption that change can occur. The boot is on the other foot.

This discussion has focused on crisis tendencies on the large scale. It is also possible for crisis tendencies to emerge on the small scale – in personal life and in intimate relationships. Crisis tendencies arise when personal practice is structured around commitments which are both urgent and contradictory. The classic case is the incompatible desires and fears of the young child in the 'oedipal' crisis, which Freud thought the basis of all later neuroses. We do not have to accept Freud's theory to agree that contradictions often arise in personal life, and drive change in a person's trajectory through life.

These changes may be individual and produce nothing but eccentricity. But they may also move in parallel with other lives, and this can result in sustainable change. The Women's Liberation movement of the 1960s and 1970s was not just a public event; it was fuelled by contradictions in the personal lives of women, especially in their relations with men. Narratives by women from this movement (e.g. those collected by Barbara Laslett and Barrie Thorne, 1997) show how the similarity of these experiences was recognized and became a basis of solidarity. Their actions, in turn, stimulated changes in the trajectories of certain men. One consequence was the 'fair families' of the 1980s and 1990s, whose story has recently been explored by Barbara Risman (1998).

Since the involvement of the body in gender relations is a social process, crisis tendencies may also arise at the level of the body. Freud's classic analysis of 'hysteria' recognized precisely that: a bodily effect (e.g. a cough, or a paralysed arm) whose cause was a psychological conflict. The bodily effects may be much rougher than Dr Freud's genteel patients were used to. Asserting masculinity, in a poor neighbourhood or a factory or on the road, may result in violence, industrial injury, or road death. I noted in chapter 3 how factory work consumes the workers' bodies, and how exemplary masculinity in professional sport produces over-use, injury, and long-term bodily damage.

Crisis tendencies may even affect bodily sensations. As Lynne Segal observes in *Straight Sex* (1994), there have been many difficulties in heterosexual relations connected with the new feminism. They are not necessarily produced by feminism – arguably, by the same crisis tendencies that gave rise to feminism. Similarly, the violations of gender boundaries in transsexuality do not just occur in people's heads. They often involve bodily sensations such as hallucinations of a body of the other sex, or a sensation of being trapped within the wrong body – see, for instance, Katherine Cummings' account of her transsexual experience in *Katherine's Diary* (1992).

Thus crisis tendencies in gender emerge on the large scale and on the small. All four structures contain crisis tendencies; but they are not the same tendencies, and they do not necessarily develop at the same pace or mature at the same time. There is, thus, complexity and unevenness in the process of historical change. It is not surprising that gender orders are far from homogeneous, and that gender politics are complicated and turbulent.

5

Gender in Personal Life

To most people being a 'man' or a 'woman' is above all a matter of personal experience. It is something involved in the way we grow up, the way we conduct family life and sexual relationships, the way we present ourselves, and see ourselves, in everyday situations. In this chapter I will examine some issues that arise in this intimate, personal realm, and reflect on how to understand what happens here.

Growing up gendered

When 'sex role' theory provided the main framework for discussion of gender, there was a fairly straightforward account of how people acquired gender. Babies were, from the start, called either female or male – labelled by the famous pink and blue baby clothes. Blue babies were expected to behave differently from pink babies – rougher and tougher, more demanding, aggressive and vigorous. In time they were given toy guns, footballs, and computer games. The pink babies, by contrast, were expected to be more passive and compliant, also prettier. As they grew older they were dressed in frilly clothes, given dolls and makeup kits, told to take care of their appearance and be polite and agreeable.

In the fullness of time the former blue babies would be taught to run cars and solve mathematical equations, to compete in the marketplace and earn a living, and to pursue former pink babies. The former pink babies would be taught to cook, to be good at human relations, to do what they were told, and to make themselves attractive to the former blue babies.

Put more formally, the idea was that sex roles were acquired by 'socialization'. Various 'agencies of socialization', notably the family, the school, the peer group and the mass media, took the growing child in hand. Through an immense number of small interactions, these agencies conveyed to the girl or the boy what were the social 'norms' or expectations for her or his behaviour. This could be done by imitating admired 'role models', such as a father might be for a boy; or it could be done piecemeal. Compliance with the norms would lead to rewards, or 'positive sanctions': smiles from mother, approval from friends, good marks at school, success in the dating game, appointment to a good job. Nonconformity or deviance would lead to negative sanctions, all the way from frowns and cross voices to getting beaten up or sent to gaol.

With this mixture of positive and negative reinforcement, most children would learn the gender-appropriate behaviour as they grew up. They would eventually do it automatically, and come to think of themselves as the kind of people they were supposed to be. They would actually develop the traits of character the society thought appropriate for women or for men, and thus 'internalize' the norms. As fully socialized members of society, they would in turn apply negative sanctions to deviants, and convey the norms to the next generation. The sex role system thus seemed to have an inbuilt stabilizing mechanism, and would reproduce itself over time. Of course the process could go wrong, for instance if fathers disappeared from families and boys lacked role models, which would probably lead to deviance.

There is something to be said for this story of how gender is acquired, but there are also severe problems with it; so severe, in fact, that the 'socialization' model should be abandoned.

First, there is not just one 'sex role' for boys and one other for girls. There are *multiple* patterns of masculinity and femininity in contemporary societies. These result partly from class differences (e.g. business masculinity vs. manual craftsmen's masculinity) and the ethnic pluralism of modern societies (e.g. different traditions about wife/husband relations among Chinese-Americans, African-Americans, and Anglo-Americans, or between Turkish immigrants and native-born Germans). But multiple patterns also arise within gender relations, through the contradictions and dynamics discussed in chapter 4.

Second, the socialization model supposes that learning gender is a matter of acquiring *traits*, that is, regularities of character that will produce regularities of behaviour. Sex role theory, basically, is a version of the 'difference' model of gender discussed in chapter 3. But as we saw in chapter 3, major differences in traits between women and men (also girls and boys) are hard to detect. Even when the scales used by psychologists detect some average differences between women and men, they are slight in comparison with the variation among women, and among men. It is clear that the business of growing up and learning about gender cannot be just a matter of internalizing role norms.

Third, the 'socialization' model pictures the learner as passive. In this model active agencies transmit role norms to a passive learner, whose only task is to internalize what he or she is given. When we turn to real situations where gender learning is going on, they do not look much like this. Consider the American elementary schools studied by Barrie Thorne (chapter 2). The boys and girls here are not lying back and letting the gender norms wash over them. They are constantly active in the matter. They take up gender divisions supplied by adults, sometimes accept them, and sometimes don't. They set up their own gender divisions in the playground, and then disrupt them. They try out gendered self-presentations (e.g. the older girls put on lip gloss), and some of them try cross-gender presentations (e.g. girls being sporty or rough). They complain, joke, fantasize and question about gender matters. Similar energy and activity appear in other studies of gender learning, such as the British upper secondary students described by Máirtín Mac an Ghaill in *The Making of Men* (1994).

The socialization model seems to miss the *pleasure* which is obvious in much gender learning, the enthusiasm with which young people take up gender symbolism (e.g. sexy clothes) and construct gendered relations (e.g. teenage dating). Nor does it give much insight into the *resistance* which many young people put up to hegemonic definitions of gender: the boys who hate sport, the girls who want to be astronauts, the teenagers who recognize themselves as gay. It also seems to miss the *difficulty* which is involved in constructing identities and working out patterns of conduct in a gender order marked by power, violence and alienated sexualities. Sue Lees' disturbing study of fifteen- and sixteen-year-old girls in Britain, *Losing Out* (1986), showed almost intolerable dilemmas about sexual reputation in dealing with boys who share a misogynist culture. As one girl remarked: 'It's a vicious circle. If you don't like them, then they'll call you a tight bitch. If you go with them they'll call you a slag afterwards.' Thinking about the presentation of women in recent popular music as 'whores' and 'bitches', it is clear this dilemma is not unusual.

The fourth problem with the socialization model is that it recognizes just one direction of learning – toward the sex role norms. It is difficult, in such a framework, to understand the changes of direction that often appear in a young person's life, coming apparently from nowhere – that is, nowhere outside the person. Developmental crises sometimes occur, with a sudden change in gender practice. There can be a shift of attachment from mother to father, a new level of aggression, a sudden burst of sexual activity, a turning away from girls or boys. Rather than just failing to 'internalize' the gender patterns of her/his parents, a young person may vehemently reject them, criticize their political or human inadequacy, and launch out on a search for something different.

This aspect of human development is much better understood by psychoanalysis than by role theory. The view of growth first worked out in Freud's case studies emphasizes conflict and contradiction. Freud recognized that a person is often developing in different directions at the same time – for instance at unconscious and conscious levels. Whether or not we accept the models put forward by contemporary schools of psychoanalysis (they remain deeply divided), this insight seems important.

A better account of how we acquire gender must therefore recognize both the contradictions of development, and the fact that learners are active, not passive. People growing up in a gendered society unavoidably encounter gender relations, and actively participate in them. This participation is disorganized to some extent, because the patterns of their lives are not yet settled. Hence the element of anarchy in 'gender play', as Thorne describes it, with children dodging in and out of gender patterns. This anarchy can reappear later in life if there is an attempt to unlearn or re-learn gender patterns, where it may be experienced as more terrifying – gender vertigo rather than gender play.

Chapter 3 argued that we must recognize the agency of bodies in the social world, and this is true in the learning of gender. The active learner is embodied. The pleasure involved in learning gender is to some extent a bodily pleasure, pleasure in the body's appearance and in the body's performance. Bodily changes such as menarche, first ejaculation, the 'breaking' of a boy's voice and the development of a girl's breasts, are often important in the development of gender. Their meanings are nevertheless ambiguous until they are given definition by the society's gender symbolism.

Because gender practice involves bodies but is not biologically determined, the gender practice being learned may actually be hostile to bodies' physical well-being. Young men in the United States and Australia, enacting their fresh-minted masculinities on the roads, die in appalling numbers, at a rate four times higher than young women. A large number of adolescent girls and young women go in for dieting, in an attempt to maintain their heterosexual attractiveness. For a certain percentage this escalates into life-threatening anorexia. Older men sometimes die of diseases that could be cured, because they have learnt it is unmanly to admit pain and request help.

Embodied learners encounter the gender regimes (as defined in chapter 4) of the institutions they come in contact with. The socialization model was right about the importance of the family, the school, and the media in children's lives, but rarely acknowledged the internal complexity of these institutions. Conflicting models and messages are likely. In a school, the teachers present a range of different patterns of masculinity and femininity to the children, simply as a result of the diversity in their own lives. The children are likely to pick up some of the gender politics among their elders – tensions, divisions and alliances. Their elders, in turn, may be divided about gender issues in their treatment of the children. Even in a two-parent family, there is room for argument about how to bring up a girl or a boy.

Further, the same experience may be interpreted in different ways. For instance, a boy growing up in a situation of domestic violence, where his father often bashes his mother, may incorporate violence towards women into his own repertoire of masculinity. Many do; it is common for men convicted of wife abuse to describe domestic violence in their own childhood. But the boy may also react against it out of terror (especially as violence against wives often goes together with violence against children), or may side with his mother and reach for a totally different relationship with women in his own life.

Institutions do not mechanically determine young people's learning. But they do shape the consequences of what young people do – the risks they run, the recognition they get, the networks they gain access to, the penalties they pay. For instance, adopting a particular pattern of masculinity may strongly affect the academic success a boy experiences in school, and thus the occupational paths open to him later. A pattern of combative, physically assertive masculine display, the 'protest masculinity' which is familiar in working-class schools, may result in major conflict with teachers, disruption to learning, sometimes violence and expulsion from school. On the other hand there are patterns of masculinity, more familiar in elite schools, which are equally competitive but pursue competition through the channels provided by the school. Boys developing this pattern of masculinity are likely to be headed for academic success and professional careers. (For a useful survey of boys' differing relations to school see *Uncertain Masculinities*, by Mike O'Donnell and Sue Sharpe, 2000.)

As children grapple with their places in a gendered world, they are not, for the most part, internalizing gender-specific behaviours. (As I noted in chapter 3, strictly gender-specific behaviours are rare.) Children are, much more importantly, learning how gender relations work, and how to navigate among them.

Much of young people's learning about gender is learning *gender competence* in this sense. Young people learn how to negotiate the gender order. They learn how to adopt a certain gender identity and produce a certain gender performance. They also learn how to distance themselves from a given gender identity, how to joke about their own performance. Most boys and girls fail to match gender ideals – ideals of handsomeness, beauty, skill, achievement or recognition. But most of them cope. They eventually 'know how to go on', to borrow Wittgenstein's famous phrase.

It is helpful to think of active learning as involving a commitment of oneself in a particular direction. The learner does not simply absorb what is to be learnt; the learner engages with it, moves forward in life in a particular direction. The pleasure in gender learning, already mentioned, is the pleasure of creativity and movement. Gender learning can occur at any moment that a young person encounters gender relations in the situations of everyday life, and grapples with those situations. It is not usually planned, and it need not be explicitly named as gender – it may be thought of as 'sports I enjoy', 'fights with my parents', 'jobs I am suited for', etc.

This is not to say gender learning is shapeless. From early in the process, what is learnt is likely to be connected with other pieces of learning, and made into wholes. Children learn about, and shape in their own lives, patterns of practice – the *configurations* of gender practice in personal life that we call 'femininity' and 'masculinity'.

Gender configurations, being patterns of activity, are not static. (This is one reason why the attempts by some psychologists to capture masculinity and femininity with standardized paper-and-pencil scales do not work very well.) The process of engaging with a situation, moving forward, happens not just at the level of particular pieces of learning, it also happens on the larger scale of a whole life. Masculinity and femininity are 'projects', to use a term suggested by the philosopher Jean-Paul Sartre (1968). They are patterns of a life-course projected from the present into the future, bringing new conditions or events into existence which were not there before.

Seeing gender learning as the creation of *gender projects* makes it possible to acknowledge both the agency of the learner and the intractability of gender structures. Gender patterns develop in personal life as a series of encounters with the constraints and possibilities of the existing gender order. In these encounters the learner improvises, copies, creates, and thus develops characteristic strategies for handling situations in which gender relations are present – learns 'how to go on' in particular ways. Over time, especially if the strategies are successful, they become settled, crystallizing as specific patterns of femininity or masculinity.

The existing structure of power, division of labour, etc. mean that some strategies are more likely than others to get results. So there is likely to be overlap in the gender projects, a degree of social standardization of individual lives. We might call these common *trajectories* of gender formation. They are what researchers pick up as patterns of 'masculinity' or 'femininity' in life-history and ethnographic research.

Gender projects are not one-dimensional or smooth. A young person may be developing two or more different, and perhaps conflicting, gender strategies at the same time. One thinks of the footballer who also writes poetry, the teenage sexpot who is also studying hard for university. Such conflicts are very familiar in adolescence, as teenagers try out one strategy after another. They can also continue into adulthood. The well-known novel *Regeneration* by Pat Barker (1992), set in the First World War, has such a conflict as a central theme. In it the poet Siegfried Sassoon faces an intolerable tension between two commitments: his conventional masculine commitment as a soldier to stand by his comrades and continue fighting, and his sense of care and responsibility to protest against a war which he has come to see as an outrage and atrocity.

The complexity or contradictoriness of gender relations, as seen in chapter 4, may themselves produce conflict in the course of growing up. The classic example is the 'oedipus complex' identified by Freud in early childhood, arising from the clash between emotional attachment to the mother and to the father. Another familiar example, in adolescence, is the conflict between loyalty to a same-gender 'peer group' of friends, and cross-gender attachment to a boyfriend or a girlfriend. Conflict may also develop when a young person's gender practice violates or resists convention. This resistance may find social support, as Huey Brown did (chapter 2), because there was an existing network of same-sex relationships in Nullangardie which he was able to find. But a young person may not find such support, resulting in loneliness and fear; this is a significant issue for telephone counselling services such as suicide prevention hotlines.

In the typical case, Freud considered, the oedipal crisis does get resolved. Through its resolution, the child moves on to a new stage of development. We need not agree with Freud's focus on the oedipus complex to agree with the broader argument. A life-history, and a gender project within a life-history, does not unfold seamlessly. It involves a number of distinct *moments* or *stages*, in which different gender commitments are made, different strategies are adopted, or different resolutions of gender issues are achieved.

Let me give as an example my own research with a small group of men in the Australian 'green' movement (Connell 1995: ch. 5). Most of them grew up in homes with a conventional gender division of labour, and in childhood and adolescence began to make a commitment to hegemonic masculinity. But this moment of engagement was followed by a moment of negation, as they began to distance themselves from hegemonic masculinity, for a variety of reasons including family conflict. Most then, in the counter-culture or in the green movement, encountered feminism and were obliged to confront gender issues head-on: this was a moment of separation from hegemonic masculinity. That was where some remained at the time we interviewed them. Some, however, had moved on to a moment of contestation, starting a political project of reforming masculinity and committing themselves to gender equality.

I do not believe there is a standard set of stages in gender formation – though a number of psychologists, from Freud on, have thought there are. What we know about the diversity of gender orders makes it unlikely that there are universal rules for the way gender is learnt. Perhaps the nearest thing to a universal rule is the fact of qualitative change. Any particular gender project, for an individual or a group in their distinct historical setting, is likely to involve points of transition, different moments of development. No life-course is mechanically determined by its point of origin.

The diversity of masculinities and femininities evident in a great deal of gender research implies different trajectories of gender formation. Class inequalities, ethnic diversity, regional difference, national origin and migration create different experiences of childhood. Ethnographies of childhood such as the California Childhoods Project (Thorne et al. forthcoming) clearly show this diversity of paths. The gender regimes of institutions allow different encounters with the gender order prevailing among adults. There may also be conflict among adults over gender issues for children: parents may criticize sex and violence in the media, churches may criticize laxness among parents, the media poke fun at the churches . . . .

The diversity of trajectories is well shown in a recent British study, Gillian Dunne's *Lesbian Lifestyles* (1997), which looks at the childhoods of women who are *not* heterosexual in adulthood. Some served an 'apprenticeship' to conventional femininity, some were tomboys; some grew up in families with a conventional division of labour, some in egalitarian homes. Dunne emphasizes the agency of the girls in responding to these experiences. But she also notes the intractability of the gender order. As they moved into adolescence, where the 'romance' and 'dating' culture ruled, many of the girls found the middle ground in gender relations, which they had previously occupied, disappearing beneath their feet. As one woman, Connie, recalls:

The whole thing changed, suddenly they became totally different people. I thought what is this thing that happens to everyone else and doesn't happen to me? . . . I didn't know how to behave, quite honestly. They all seemed to have this secret code that they all learned, and I didn't. They all knew how to behave at discos, and I would sit pinned to the wall terrified. Where did they learn this? I didn't have it. It was some sort of pattern of social behaviour that everyone fell into, and I didn't have it – God! . . . The big 'goo goo' eyes came out, the painted faces, and the frocks, and all that stuff, and the act, the peacock act, basically attracting. At 12, they would stop being your mate that you had known, and suddenly they would become this minor adult, doing something that you didn't understand. They would suddenly be – Oh! With the boys, flirting big eyes, all that sort of thing; it didn't seem right for me, I could never do it.

Diversity does not mean chaos. Children's gender strategies intersect, as Thorne's school ethnography (chapter 2) shows. They deal with the same institutions and with overlapping groups of adults. One of the key competencies children learn is to know what are the prevailing masculinities and femininities in the adult world. Whatever ideology prevails in the gender order, children grow up under its shadow. They may not embrace it, but they cannot forget it. Consider Harriet Brown's trajectory (chapter 2): wildly aberrant for a working-class boy in some respects, but still reaching for a settled couple relationship that was in some respects a conventional marriage.

It is difficult to make a complete break with the gender patterns one has grown up with. With this in mind, Gay Liberation activists spoke of 'self-oppression' among gay men. A heterosexual version of the same dilemma is presented in Doris Lessing's famous novel *The Golden*

Notebook (1962). Lessing pictures her heroines Anna and Molly as trying to conduct independent lives as 'free women', consistent with the principles of British left-wing politics. But they find their autonomy constantly undermined by their emotional need for relationship with a man. Their political experience, even their financial independence, makes no difference.

Yet the gender order does change, and this makes possible new personal trajectories, new paths of learning. Young women growing up in communities influenced by the Women's Liberation movement have their own dilemmas about jobs, marriage and children, as can be seen in the autobiographies collected by Jocelynne Scutt in *Growing up Feminist* (1985). But they do not face the same impasse as women of Doris Lessing's generation.

There is some evidence that belief in gender equality has also spread among younger men. Witness the recent national study of men in Germany by Zulehner and Volz (1998), where men below fifty endorse a gender-equal model of family life, and reject 'traditional' norms, about twice as often as men above fifty. But communities with a consistently egalitarian view of gender are rare, and as the case of Eastern Europe shows (chapter 2), societies can move in the other direction. To understand the forces shaping paths of gender development we have to move outward from personal life to gender patterns in larger arenas. This is the subject of chapter 6.

Gender identity

Perhaps the commonest way of understanding the presence of gender in personal life is through the concept of 'gender identity'. The term 'identity' has a long history in philosophy and literature, and has gone through a curious shift in meaning.

When the word was taken over from late Latin into English, about the sixteenth century, it was a philosophical term that meant exact agreement, sameness. It was used when a writer wanted to refer to a thing or person remaining the same over time, or despite different circumstances. The philosopher John Locke, for instance, used the term that way in his famous book *On Human Understanding*. Initially, then, the concept of 'identity' was one of a family of philosophical and religious terms that expressed the theme of unity. By the nineteenth century the term 'identity' had become thoroughly naturalized in English and was used in literature as well as philosophy and mathematics. It was still generally used with the meaning of 'sameness', though sometimes in the sense of personal existence, or to emphasize who I am as against who I am not.

By the late nineteenth century, however, 'who I am' had become more and more of a problem for the speakers of European languages. The feudal social order was dead, replaced by a restless capitalism, gigantic new cities, enormous labour migrations and turbulent working classes. A radical workers' movement challenged class division in the name of human equality. At the same time, global empires brought Europeans and North Americans face to face with radically different cultures, and urgently posed the question of human sameness and difference. Was the Cheyenne or the Zulu the white man's brother? Was the Australian Aboriginal, or the Bengali, on the same plane as the British conqueror? Some said yes; but more and more voices among the conquerors said no. A new language of 'race' emerged during the nineteenth century to deny human unity.

A shift was simultaneously occurring in conceptions of gender. Men and women had traditionally been thought of as the same kind of being (though one a more perfect version of it than the other). Western culture increasingly rejected this view and defined men and women as different in nature, even opposites (Laqueur 1990). Men and women were irrevocably assigned to 'separate spheres' suited to their different natures. There was a material basis for this. Fascinating archaeological research has traced the physical separation of workplace from domestic life, and the gradual segregation of cities like New York on gender as well as class lines (Wall 1994). Entrenched in the very stones of the city, the belief in separate spheres became so powerful that it was accepted even by most nineteenth-century feminists.

Thus Western bourgeois culture – now the dominant culture in the world – came to include a powerful ideology of innate differences between people. These were supposed to be differences of character as well as physical type, and were reflected in the hierarchies of class, race and gender. Yet this belief was under challenge as soon as it was formulated. It was challenged by anti-colonial intellectuals such as Mohandas Gandhi, who argued against the idea of inherited or acquired superiority on the grounds that 'all have the same soul'. Belief in fixed differences was challenged in another way by the radical psychology of Sigmund Freud. Freud came to see adult personalities as being *by necessity* internally divided and full of conflict. Freud did not share Gandhi's idea of all people having the 'same soul'. Rather, he saw the diversity of adult mental life – including feminine and masculine conduct, heterosexuality and homosexuality – as the outcomes of distinctive life-histories, leading to different mental makeups.

Freud's conflictual view of personality was developed in varying ways by his argumentative followers, especially Alfred Adler. A socialist doctor in Vienna, Adler was concerned with the health of the working class, and was also influenced by the women's movement of the day. This background led him to the view that one's social location, especially one's degree of social power, was a crucial cause of personal histories and psychological conflicts. In a remarkable early synthesis of feminist and psychoanalytic ideas, Adler suggested that the core of the neuroses was not repressed sexuality, as Freud thought, but the 'masculine protest'. This was a distorted striving for superiority, rooted in the small child's emotional interpretation of men's power, and women's subordination, within the family. The ultimate answer to the neuroses produced by a gender-divided society, Adler (1927) later came to believe, was to develop a unifying sense of social responsibility and mutual obligation.

These insights became the basis of the twentieth century's most influential statement about identity. Erik Erikson's famous *Childhood and Society* (1950) interpreted a range of modern personal, social and political problems as difficulties in achieving identity. 'The study of identity, then, becomes as strategic in our time as the study of sexuality was in Freud's time' (Erikson 1950: 242). Erikson's concept of personal identity was based on the Freudian insight that adult personality is formed by a long, conflict-ridden process of growth.

But where Freud had focused on conflicts involving unconscious agencies of the mind (the 'id' and the 'superego'), Erikson emphasized the conscious agency, the 'ego'. The ego is the mental agency involved in transactions with the outside world, the agency where the conscious sense of self is located. To Erikson the term 'identity' meant the coherence of the psychological mechanisms by which the ego handles the pressures that impinge on it – from the unconscious mind, on the one side, and the outside world, on the other. This feat of balance, if successful, is registered in a stable sense of self. Thus the question 'who am I?' is, in principle, answered by the ego's success in mastering the trials and tribulations of psychological development. This was, Erikson thought, a particularly important issue in one stage of development, adolescence. This idea has led to a great deal of popular discussion of adolescence as a 'search for identity'.

The key application of this concept to gender was made by the American psychiatrist Robert Stoller (1968), who altered it in two ways. First, the 'core gender identity' that Stoller saw as the basis of adult personality was supposed to be formed very early in life – in the first two or three years – not in adolescence. Second, the concept of identity acquired a different frame of reference. Erikson referred to the integration of the ego as a whole. Stoller's conception was much more specific. To talk of 'gender identity' is to talk only of *one aspect* of the person – her or his involvement in gender relations or sexual practice.

To Stoller this narrower focus did not matter because he assumed that the integration of the personality as a whole *was* largely focused on the sense of being a male or a female. But on any other view of personality and social process, an exclusive focus on gender is a problem. We can speak just as meaningfully of 'racial identity', 'generational identity' or 'class identity'. If we acknowledge the 'constant interweaving' (Bottomley 1992) of these social relations, we *must* attend to these other forms of identity in order to understand gender identity. The concept of 'identity' formulated by Stoller thus leads towards a conception of identity as inherently *plural* rather than unitary.

A model of identity built on gender dichotomy was more easily accepted by the 1970s because of the growth of American feminist research emphasizing gender difference in the rearing of children. The most influential statement of this point was Nancy Chodorow's *The Reproduction of Mothering* (1978).

Chodorow's argument linked the gender division of labour, which assigned the task of caring for babies and infants exclusively to women, with the paths of development for girls and boys which resulted from their different emotional situations in early childhood. Girls, brought up by a parent of their own gender, tend to have less distinct ego boundaries. When they grow up they have a stronger motivation for nurturing children. Boys, pushed towards separation from a mother responding to the gender distinction, tend to have an earlier discontinuity or break in development. They have more difficulty in establishing gender identity, and stronger boundaries to the self in adulthood.

The gender division of labour in childcare is a fact, part of the broad division of labour discussed in chapter 4. Though it has been well established that men *can* 'mother' (Risman 1986), it is still the case that, in contemporary Western society, few of them do. But the reasons for this may be economic rather than psychological. In Norway, where the cost of losing a man's wage has been sharply reduced by the introduction of a 'Father's Quota' of paid parental leave, some 70 per cent of eligible men take up their entitlement and are present as carers in the first month of their child's life (Gender Equality Ombudsman 1997). There has also been increased recognition – by Chodorow (1994) among others – that we do not find dichotomous gender patterns in adult personalities. As the psychological 'sex difference' research discussed above in chapter 3 indicates, the outcomes of child development are curiously un-dichotomous.

Social researchers too have increasingly recognized variation within the gender categories. This is plain in the recent research on masculinity. In contrast to the way '*the* male role' was discussed in the 1970s, it has become common to speak of 'masculinities' in the plural. There is considerable diversity between cultures in their constructions of gender for men. This can readily be seen by comparing recent descriptions of masculinities in Latin America, the Middle East, and southern Africa (Gutmann 2001, Ghoussoub and Sinclair-Webb 2000, Morrell 2001). There is also considerable evidence that there are multiple masculinities within the same culture, even within the same institution, peer group or workplace. A striking example is Douglas Foley's (1990) ethnography of a high school in a Texas country town in the USA. Here the interplay of gender, class and ethnicity constructs several versions of masculinity. There is the dominant group of Anglo 'jocks', anti-authoritarian Mexican-American 'vatos', and the group which Foley calls ironically the 'silent majority'.

The trend has therefore been to speak of multiple gender and sexual identities. Some psychologists, for instance, have mapped out the stages of acquisition of a 'homosexual identity' (Troiden 1989) as one among a number of possible sexual identities in modern society. But there is a significant shift of ground in moving from the concept of 'identity' to the concept of 'gender identity' or 'sexual identity'. With the categories seeming more and more complex, the concept of identity has increasingly been used to name claims made by individuals about who or what they are.

This is closely related to the growth (especially in the United States) of 'identity politics', since the decline of socialist and class-based movements which had universal objectives. One becomes a member of a social movement by claiming the identity (as Black, as a woman, as lesbian, etc.) that the movement represents. 'Queer' politics takes the process a step further. Queer activists have challenged taken-for-granted communities by emphasizing their diversity: highlighting the presence of Black lesbians in white-dominated lesbian communities, for instance. At the extreme, the concept of identity becomes a way of naming one's uniqueness, rather than naming what is shared.

Even the well-researched 'identities' of gender and sexuality prove, on close examination, to be less solid than we might think. Arne Nilsson's (1998) beautifully crafted study of homosexual history in the Swedish city of Göteborg identifies three ways of being homosexual: 'so', commonly a bit effeminate; 'real men', often working-class youth; and 'fjollor', flamboyant queens. Three identities, perhaps? But Nilsson also shows how the patterns of homosexual life grew out of the structure of the industrial and maritime city. Among the conditions shaping sexuality were crowded housing, a sharp gender division of labour, high density of men in public spaces, a non-respectable working-class street life, connections to other cities via the shipping trade, certain patterns of policing, and the poverty of many young men, who might enter homosexual relationships for a period and then move on.

The distinctive forms of homosexual practice changed as these conditions changed. The 1950s saw rising affluence in Sweden, suburban working-class housing, the growth of the welfare state, and moral panics about the seduction of youth. A sharper cultural distinction between heterosexual and homosexual people followed the increasing privacy of sexual conduct itself. Thus the configurations of sexual and social practice which might easily be read as 'identities' were dependent on historically transitory social conditions, and for many participants were only a limited part of their whole sexual life-history.

Given such problems with the idea of 'identity', is the concept worth anything at all? Certainly the word has been massively over-used. It often serves merely as a pretentious synonym for self, reputation, or social standing.

In some cases, to use the term 'identity' for a configuration of gender or sexual practice may be actively misleading. Guy Hocquenghem (1972), one of the most brilliant theorists of Gay Liberation, argued that homosexual desire is *in principle* inchoate, anarchic, an impersonal flux not a personal unity. Homosexual desire is desire that escapes being 'oedipalized', that is, organized by the patriarchal social order. Homosexuality is, in a sense, the opposite of an identity, being desire and practice that cannot be welded into a unity. I think his argument does not go far enough. A great deal of *heterosexual* desire also fails to be 'oedipalized'. Heterosexual desire, too, is often perverse, transitory, unbounded, and pushes against the social authority that constructs fixed positions and bounded identities in a heterosexual order. As Lynne Segal puts it in *Straight Sex* (1994: 254–5): 'Sexual relations are perhaps the most fraught and troubling of all social relations precisely because, especially when heterosexual, they so often *threaten* rather than confirm gender polarity.' For instance, it is precisely in sex that heterosexual men are most likely to experience dependence, uncertainty, passivity and – quite simply – shared experience with women.

To Erikson there was never any doubt that it was desirable to have a unified identity. He saw that as a task to be accomplished in the course of growing up. Most other people who have written about 'identity' have also assumed that everybody ought to have one. But is this really so desirable? Some identities I can think of are pretty revolting – at least in their consequences for others.

To weld one's personality into a united whole is to refuse internal diversity and openness. It may also be to refuse change. Major reform in gender relations may well require a de-structuring of the self, an experience of gender vertigo, as part of the process. I have documented this for a group of men in the Australian 'green' movement who were trying to change traditional masculinity (Connell 1995: ch. 5). The American sociologist Barbara Risman (1998) has found a comparable experience in 'fair families' in the United States. There is something to be said for living with contradictions, rather than trying to erase them.

Gender and sexualities

Sexuality is the realm of intimate contact where particularly strong emotional bonds are forged. Yet on this very territory a trend towards fragmentation and alienation has emerged. The leading contemporary theorist of sexuality, the British historian Jeffrey Weeks (1986), argues convincingly that the 'speciation' of sexuality, the diversification of practices, subcultures and identities, is characteristic of the present moment.

Sexual matters have to be dealt with in all cultures, but they may be dealt with in very different ways. The anthropologist Kalpana Ram (1991) notes how the language in which sexual matters are spoken of, among the Mukkuvar people of south India, makes women's sexuality inseparable from questions of auspiciousness and fertility, representing a kind of social prosperity. By contrast, Christianity long valued chastity above sexual fulfilment. A vow of chastity was a basic part of being a monk or nun. Chastity for priests was originally an ideal, that was turned into a rule during the great reform of the medieval church by Pope Gregory VII.

In chapter 4 I noted that the distinction between 'homosexual' and 'heterosexual' is a key to the structure of emotional attachments in contemporary Western society. This distinction, so important now, is relatively recent. In medieval and early modern Europe, specific homosexual acts were often defined as shameful or criminal, but were lumped together with other disruptions of religion or social order, like blasphemy. They were not thought to define a particular kind of person, just a particular kind of sin, which anyone, if carried away by lust and pride, might commit (Greenberg 1988). By the eighteenth century, in the booming commercial cities of Western Europe, networks of men involved in same-sex activity had formed and they began to be seen as a distinctive group. Changed laws, in the late nineteenth century, criminalized homosexual behaviour generally and led to regular police surveillance and arrests.

At about the same time homosexuality was redefined as a medical condition. This was part of an expansion of the medical idea of 'pathology' to include sexual behaviour, a shift that was brought to fruition by the Austrian doctor Richard von Krafft-Ebing. His medico-legal treatise *Psychopathia Sexualis* (1885) is one of the founding documents of modern sexology and sex law reform, and became a best-seller. There is debate among historians as to how far a sexual subculture had already been created in European cities. But there can be little doubt about the importance of legal and medical discourses in shaping the modern category of 'the homosexual' (Weeks 1977).

This is the most important, but not the only, case of diversification. New categories of sexuality, and new erotic objects, have been emerging in a ferment. In major cities there is now a considerable range of sexual subcultures, with bars, clubs, shops, mail and telephone services catering for different (though often overlapping) interests: leather scenes, sadomasochistic, fetishistic, cross-dressing, cross-age, cross-ethnic, bondage, and so on. It is possible to trace in fine detail the construction of particular sexual subcultures. This has been done by Gayle Rubin (1991) for a famous 'fisting' venue in San Francisco, describing in remarkable detail the setting, the participants, the styles of sexuality, the leading personalities, the economic and political history of the venue.

There is also a 'speciation' within heterosexuality. Here the interplay of two of the structures of gender, emotional attachment and power relations, is crucial. The power of heterosexual men in a patriarchal system makes it possible to treat women as objects in a way that not only depersonalizes desire but practically dismembers their bodies.

Folklore among heterosexual men has long distinguished 'leg men' from 'tit men'. Current heterosexual pornography shows an immense development of this specialization. Magazines and videos are now readily available in the shops which make specialized appeals to men's sexual interest in big breasts, big buttocks, shaved genitals; very young women, very fat women; white, Black and 'Asian' women; women dressed as nurses, schoolgirls, schoolmistresses, police; disabled women (e.g. amputees); women wearing high heels and lingerie; women penetrated by vegetables, animals or objects. It seems that the commodification of men's sexuality has gone hand-in-hand with a strong fetishization of desire. The body is treated as a *thing* rather than a person.

This is not the only form of male heterosexuality – things would be very depressing if it were. Yet the advertising, music and fashion industries have increasingly picked up themes from pornography: for instance Madonna's music videos, Versace and Gaultier clothing, and many current advertising campaigns. Commodified sex in the form of prostitution, whose clients are almost exclusively men, has been re-established in major Western cities. International sex tourism has become an important industry for developing countries such as Thailand. In sex tourism even elementary communication as persons is usually ruled out by language barriers. It seems that an alienated, fetishized spectrum of male heterosexual desire has emerged as a significant element of the current gender order.

We usually think of our sexual desire in a quite different way, as an inherent or natural part of our makeup. Theorists of sexuality have often shared that assumption. Versions of sexuality as a natural drive can be found in Darwin, Freud, the anthropologist Malinowski, the philosopher Marcuse. Many followers of Freud understood human psychology as the outcome of a clash between natural sexual urge and social repression. Even the arch-empiricist Alfred Kinsey, the insect specialist who became the most famous survey researcher on human sexuality, shared the notion of a robust, hedonistic, natural urge, which found varying expression according to social approval or prohibition (De Cecco 1990).

The whole framework that contrasts natural urge with social prohibition or distortion was dramatically rejected in the 1970s. Similar stances were taken by Foucault in France, and by the sociologists of the Kinsey Institute in the United States (Gagnon and Simon 1974), who developed the idea of sexual 'scripts'.

John Gagnon and William Simon's conception of sexual scripts is, essentially, an application of the 'role' notions that were very widespread in social psychology from the 1950s to the 1970s. The logic is like that of the 'sex role' concept, and the descriptive detail in their model of the normative heterosexual life-cycle in the United States (Gagnon and Simon 1974: 100–3) has a large overlap with the sex role literature of the day.

Foucault's celebrated *History of Sexuality*, *Volume I* (1980) offered a vehement critique of the 'repressive hypothesis'. The alternative it suggests is more subtle than Gagnon and Simon's notion of 'scripts'. Foucault argued that society did not repress sexuality, which simply does not exist as an entity in nature. Rather, social discourses *constituted* sexuality as a cultural form, in the historical transition to modernity. This established a new form of power over bodies and their pleasures, a power exercised not only by law but also by medicine, psychotherapy, and sexology itself. Foucault's argument expanded social constructionism to new territory, and has been followed by a flood of research on discourses of sexuality and the production of sexual identities, which still shows little sign of abating.

These were important advances; but they had problems. Gender is, notoriously, absent from Foucault's theoretical universe. Gender is found in scripting theory mainly in the very simplified form of 'sex roles', or dichotomous sexual scripts. Social constructionist accounts also seem to have difficulties understanding the bodily dimension of sexuality. It often seems to be bodily processes and products – arousal, orgasm, pregnancy and birth, menarche and menopause, tumescence and detumescence, semen, milk and sweat – that underpin the biological-determinist sense of sex as a domain of eternal repetition.

Social constructionist approaches to sexuality, as Carole Vance (1989) observes, risk drifting away from bodily experience altogether. It is important, then, to recall the argument (chapter 3 above) that the bodily processes and experiences conventionally taken to be outside history are indeed elements of social process.

This social analysis of bodies connects sexuality with the structures of gender (chapter 4). In sexual practices, bodies are drawn into social processes, but they are not drawn into a featureless world. They are drawn into a social world that is structured by gender relations. Much of their practice occurs in institutions (the family, the firm, etc.) and therefore occurs within the gender regimes of those institutions. The gender order marks out places for bodies, allocates different resources, provides interpretations. Specific patterns of sexual desire and sexual conduct arise in the distinctive locations the gender order provides, and in response to socially constructed needs (e.g. for income, for security, for parenthood).

Survey research in the United States is important in showing how the gender patterning of sexuality persists over time. Comparison of surveys done in different years, and comparison of generations within the one survey, reveal two broad trends in American heterosexual practice. One is a rising rate of sexual contact outside marriage, most notably a greater number of partners in youth, and an expansion of the sexual repertoire (especially to include oral/genital sex). The other is a gradual erosion of the 'double standard', with women's patterns becoming more like those of men.

But the convergence between women and men is far from complete. In the most elaborate of these studies, the 'new Kinsey report', women are less than half as likely as men to report coming to orgasm in heterosexual intercourse. Though the interpretation of the questions is tricky, it seems that women were more than five times as likely as men to report having been forced to do something sexual they did not want to do (Laumann et al. 1994: 333–6). American heterosexuality, it appears, still reflects gender inequality.

The most profound current changes in sexuality are not, however, in the rich industrialized countries. As shown in ethnographies such as Jeffrey Clark's (1997) study of a highland community in Papua New Guinea, the more sweeping changes are in poor countries. Sexual categories and relationships are being profoundly changed in the course of dependent capitalist 'development'.

Alison Murray's *No Money, No Honey* (1991), a study of street traders and prostitutes in the capital city of Indonesia, traces this process in an urban setting. One type of prostitution in Jakarta involves lower-class women servicing the Westernized sexuality of businessmen. The women use this trade as a way into the modernized sector of Indonesian society. Another type of prostitution involves middle-class housewives who become prostitutes on a part-time basis, without giving up their respectable identities. These women were excluded from useful employment by the patriarchal policies of the Suharto dictatorship, and found a solution in the black economy. Different class sexualities, as Murray puts it, are produced despite a standard official ideology of womanhood.

Global capitalism is also impacting on sexuality among Javanese men. Javanese society traditionally provided a space for 'banci', cross-dressing men who typically have sex with straight men. This is one of many third-gender categories found, in different forms, around the world. In contemporary Indonesia 'banci' communities are distinct from a new sexual category, 'gay' men, who have emerged in more affluent social contexts with stronger links to North American gay culture (Oetomo 1996). A similar process as far away as Brazil is documented by the ethnographer Richard Parker (1991). Parker finds a local pattern of male-to-male sexuality which is based on a strong distinction between the insertive and the receptive partner. The one who penetrates maintains his masculinity, never allows himself to be penetrated, and thus remains in a separate sexual category and is not regarded as a 'homosexual'. But this sexual pattern is also being reshaped under North American influence, specifically by a 'gay' model of reciprocal sexuality.

In this pattern, both partners are both insertive and receptive, and thus both are members of the same sexual category.

Dennis Altman (1996) makes the important observation that such cases do not involve the simple substitution of a 'Western' sexuality for a 'traditional' sexuality. Globalization involves an enormously complex interaction between sexual customs and gender regimes that are in any case diverse and divided. The result is a spectrum of sexual practices and categories, formed in contexts of cultural disruption and economic inequality.

This is strikingly shown in Thailand. According to Peter Jackson (1997), the traditional Thai sex/gender categories for males were 'phu-chai' (man, mainly heterosexual) and 'kathoey' (effeminate or cross-gender, receptive homosexual). Under the impact of international gay culture, these categories have not disappeared. Rather, they have been elaborated with a series of additions: 'bai' (bisexual), 'gay-king' (homosexual, preferring to be insertor), 'gay-queen' (usually effeminate, preferring to be receptive), and 'gay-quing' (masculine or effeminate, and sexually versatile). In this inter-cultural context, same-sex practices of sexuality, like the heterosexual sexuality discussed by Segal (see previous section), seem to undermine gender polarities.

6

Gender on the Large Scale

Most discussions of gender concern the local: personal relations, identities, motherhood and child-rearing, family life, sexuality – and their pathologies, such as prejudice, domestic violence and rape. We have already seen reasons to go beyond this. It is impossible to understand personal relations without taking into account institutions, economies, mass communications and governments. Chapter 4 outlined an approach to the structure of gender relations. This chapter applies the same approach to gender relations on the very large scale: in corporations, governments and global society.

Gender in the corporation

The corporation (also known as the 'firm' or 'company') is the dominant form of economic organization in contemporary society, the key institution of developed capitalism. Accordingly, if we are to understand the economic dimension of gender, the structure of production relations (chapter 4), we must examine the corporation.

Corporations are gendered institutions, with a gendered history. 'Companies' of merchants in early modern Europe were entirely composed of men. When ownership began to be divided up and became itself a kind of commodity, with the creation of joint-stock companies and the first stock exchanges in the seventeenth and eighteenth centuries, these too were socially defined as men's institutions. The creation of the modern form of capital was part of the historical process that created a masculinized public realm, which also included the emerging liberal state, and organs of public opinion such as the press.

This went for a long time unquestioned. When in the nineteenth century middle-class women in the rich countries challenged their exclusion from universities and the professions, there was no comparable demand for entry to business management. A discussion of middle-class gender patterns related to corporate life got under way in the United States in the 1950s. It centred on the 'man in the grey flannel suit', the conformist corporate man, and his perfectly groomed wife going crazy with boredom in a brand-new house in an affluent suburb. This gender image became a symbol of the cultural malaise of consumer capitalism, but it did not involve a critique of the corporation itself. *Managers and their Wives* (1971), a British sociological study by J. M. and R. E. Pahl, also focused on the family and career issues, not on the organizations – and simply took it for granted that managers were men.

The corporation itself only came into focus in the 1970s, when liberal and academic feminism challenged organization theory. The change is marked by the work of Rosabeth Kanter, whose *Men and Women of the Corporation* appeared in 1977. Kanter criticized the absence of gender awareness in organization research, and showed how gender issues mattered, even for the minority of women who did make it into the corporate hierarchy. Over the next two decades a series of close-focus studies of corporate life have appeared, which have vastly expanded our understanding of corporate gender regimes. Some have already been mentioned: Hochschild's (1983) study of 'emotion work' in airlines and debt agencies, and Pringle's (1989) study of secretaries.

Some of the best research has focused on the lowest rungs of the ladder, the world of manual workers in large-scale industries. The sociologist Miriam Glucksmann wrote a wonderful account of British factory life in *Women on the Line* (1982). This was based on seven months' participant observation in a motor vehicle component assembly plant, and gives a vivid picture of the corporate hierarchy, daily life on the shop floor, and the connections with home life. There was a rigid gender division of labour in this plant. Women were employed in the low-paid routine jobs only, promotion was blocked, men could get twice the wage for doing easier jobs. 'It was obvious that the only qualification you needed for a better job was to be a man.' The women were disillusioned about men, and supported each other in daily conflicts with male supervisors. But their poverty, fatigue, household demands, and the gender segregation of working-class life made effective organizing almost impossible.

An equally impressive study by a Canadian team, *Recasting Steel Labour* (Corman et al. 1993), shows entrenched gender divisions beginning to change. In this case a progressive union had supported a campaign to end the exclusion of women from the shop floor. Interviews with a sample of steelworkers and their spouses found widespread support for the equal opportunity principle, though rather less support for specific applications of it. There was less support among the men than among the women. It was clear that the totally masculine shop floor culture traditional in the steel industry was eroding. But the idea that working men were the 'breadwinners' remained strong, and undermined class solidarity between the men and the newly hired women. As it happened, the steel corporation began 'downsizing' – management jargon for laying off workers permanently – at the time of the study. The last hired were the first to go, and so most of the gains of the campaign for women's employment were lost.

The gender hierarchies are not just 'tradition'; they are in many cases deliberately introduced and actively defended. That was shown in Cynthia Cockburn's classic study of printing workers, *Brothers* (1983). David Collinson, David Knights and Margaret Collinson in *Managing to Discriminate* (1990) investigated the same issue in white-collar work. Their study in a British insurance firm similarly found job segregation and gender hierarchy sustained by the action of the men. They lay emphasis on the collective character of workplace masculinity and the interlocking of prejudices. For instance, a manager opposed to promoting women justified his hostility by the idea (possibly correct!) that the customers, also men, would not like it. The women, in worse-paid jobs with promotion blocked, became defensive and indifferent – which was of course attributed to their sex and used to justify gender segregation.

In the United States more women have reached middle management. There is now a debate about the supposed 'glass ceiling' which prevents their getting into top management. In 1991 the US Congress set up a twenty-one-person Glass Ceiling Commission to investigate the problem and recommend solutions. This is one of the few public inquiries into discrimination in business, and is interesting in many ways as a contemporary attempt at gender reform. In a set of glossy reports published in 1995, the Glass Ceiling Commission documented startling levels of exclusion of women and ethnic minority men from top management. Among the biggest corporations in the USA (the 'Fortune 1,000' and 'Fortune 500'), 97 per cent of senior managers turned out to be white, and 95 to 97 per cent were men. Of the Fortune 1,000 companies, two had women CEOs (Chief Executive Officers). (That is, one-fifth of

1 per cent of big corporations had a woman in the top job. This was cited as a sign of progress.)

The Glass Ceiling Commission (1995a, 1995b) attributed this situation to a set of 'barriers' which prevent access to 'high places'. They include: unsuitable or inadequate educational background; prejudice and bias on the part of men in power; career paths that divert women from the main promotion pipeline; poor anti-discrimination enforcement by government; inadequate information about the problem; inadequate publicity; and fear of loss among white men in middle management.

These are credible observations, though 'barriers' seems an inadequate metaphor for most of them. Evidently the reasons for the absence of women (and minority men) from top management have to do with broad features of business organizations, and deeply entrenched patterns of division in the workplace – just as the sociologists had been saying. Commenting on the prevailing culture of US business, the Commission (1995b: 34) quotes the CEO of a retail firm:

> The old-line companies are run by the white '46 long' guys who practice inappropriate male rituals that are dysfunctional to business. Male bonding through hunting, fishing and sports talk is irrelevant to business. Too much so-called 'strategic planning' takes place after the bars close – that kind of male fellowship ritual is irrelevant to business.

It may be irrelevant, the Commission remarks wryly, but it thrives. And it may not be as 'irrelevant' to the way business really works as this golden-hearted CEO would like to think.

As the remedy for all this, the Glass Ceiling Commission proposes – a change of attitude. They seek to persuade the controllers of corporations that a more 'diverse' management team would be *Good for Business* (the title of their main report) and would make US corporations more competitive. That is, they rely on the profit motive to drive a massive voluntary reconstruction of business management – somehow failing to notice that the profit motive has been operating full blast since the dawn of capitalism, so far resulting in a management group 97 per cent white and 95 per cent to 97 per cent men. There is no reason to think the picture in other industrialized countries is very different.

At the top levels of corporate management, then, there is an overwhelming majority of men, and a management culture that reflects this fact. Not any kind of man will do. Most senior managers in big business come from a restricted social background: middle- and upper-class parents, members of the dominant ethnic group, and often educated in elite private schools and elite universities.

Nevertheless managerial masculinities do change over time. The British historian Michael Roper (1994), in a fascinating book called *Masculinity and the British Organization Man since 1945*, traces changes in the management of British manufacturing firms over a generation. An older generation of managers had a hands-on relation with the production process, identified themselves closely with the firm and the quality of the product, and took a paternalistic interest in the engineering workers. With the growing power of finance capital in the British economy, a new cadre of managers has appeared, sometimes gaining power through corporate amalgamations and restructuring. They are also men, but are more oriented to accountancy and profit, less interested in technology and the product, and not very much interested in the workers. A more generic, and more ruthless, managerial masculinity has taken over.

There is every reason to think similar changes have happened elsewhere. The management textbooks and business magazines themselves say so. James Gee, Glynda Hull and Colin Lankshear (1996) explore this in their study of 'fast capitalism'. The new-model executive, according to the textbooks, is a person with few permanent commitments but a driving interest in profit opportunities for his firm and himself. He is master of general techniques of financial and organizational control, and is willing for career reasons to jump between firms – and in an age of global business, willing to jump between continents.

That is the new world above the 'glass ceiling', the world which women fighting for equal opportunity now seek to join. When Rosabeth Kanter studied women in corporations in the 1970s, she found that the social pressures they were under tended to reinforce traditional femininity. When Judy Wajcman (1999) studied both women and men managers in globally oriented British-based high-technology firms in the 1990s, she found the women were under heavy pressure to act just like the men: work the long hours, fight in the office wars, put pressure on their subordinates, and focus on profit. In order to survive in this world, the women managers had to re-structure their domestic lives so they too could shed responsibilities for childcare, cooking and housework. Wajcman found no truth in the widespread belief that women coming into management would bring a more caring, nurturant or humane style to the job. It is not surprising that she called her book *Managing Like a Man*.

What difference does managerial masculinity (whether borne by men or by women) make to the course of events? This question is difficult to answer, because most of the research is cross-sectional, looking at a sample of people or workplaces rather than looking at events. But there is a particularly interesting study by James Messerschmidt (1997), an American criminologist and masculinity researcher who became interested in corporate crime. He was able, as a result of evidence given in public inquiries, to reconstruct the corporate decision-making that led to the fatal crash of the space shuttle *Challenger* in January 1986.

Messerschmidt found that the key move – a decision to ignore weather conditions which increased the chance of failure in the 'O-rings' that sealed the shuttle's fuel system – was a conscious risk-taking, which had been debated at the time within the engineering company. The decision pitted two styles of corporate masculinity against each other. One was a technically oriented masculinity, and from this quarter the doubts had been raised. The other was a tough profit-oriented managerial masculinity which was unwilling to appear weak. The disastrous decision to go ahead with the launch reflected the organizational dominance of the tough managerial masculinity in a situation where other values, or other reasoning, could have prevailed.

From the point of view of gender justice, even from the narrower point of view of equal opportunity, the picture in top management looks bleak. A masculine culture emphasizing toughness and competitiveness prevails, and the few women who make it into top management are unlikely to change this. Among men too, only those who conform, who can 'stand the heat', are likely to be recruited. The rise of finance capital and the process of globalization (which I will discuss below) have certainly changed styles of management. They have not necessarily produced more equal or more tolerant gender regimes in business.

The state and gender

When the Democratic Party candidate won the United States presidential election of 1992, he announced that he intended to appoint an administration that 'looked like America'. Surveying the results a little later, a woman commentator remarked that Clinton's administration did look like America – men on top. Clinton in fact appointed two women cabinet members, Janet Reno as Attorney-General and Madeleine Albright as Secretary of State. But no revolution followed. All four major-party candidates in the year 2000 US presidential election were men. As mentioned in chapter 1, this is still the usual situation in politics around the world.

There are obvious reasons, then, why feminists have seen the state as a patriarchal institution, a vehicle of men's power. During the 1980s a number of attempts were made to develop a theory of the state along these lines. Its main themes can be summed up in six points:

- The state is the core of the whole structure of power relations in gender (as defined in chapter 4). Traditional theories of the state in philosophy and political science said nothing about gender because they could not see gender where only men were present, where no 'difference' was visible. But where only men are present, we are looking at a powerful gender effect – that is, the total exclusion of women!
- The state has a well-marked internal gender regime (as defined in chapter 4). There is a strong gender division of labour, with men concentrated in departments such as the military, police, infrastructure and economic agencies, women concentrated in social welfare, health and education. It is typical of modern states that the centres of state power, the top decision-making units, are heavily masculine. Though women are not excluded from policymaking, as the Canadian sociologists Judith Grant and Peta Tancred (1992) point out, women's interests tend to be represented in more peripheral agencies than men's interests.
- The state has the capacity to 'do' gender. Put more conventionally, the state generates policies concerned with gender issues. As these policies are put into effect, the state regulates gender relations in the wider society. This is not a minor aspect of what the state does. It involves many policy areas, from housing through education to criminal justice and the military, a point strongly made by the Australian sociologists Suzanne Franzway and Dianne Court (Franzway, Court and Connell 1989). A familiar example is the state's intervention in sexuality through population policies – policies which are sometimes in favour of birth control (China) and sometimes against (Singapore).
- This activity not only regulates existing gender relations. The state's activity also helps to *constitute* gender relations and form gender identities. An important example is the role of repressive laws and state-backed medicine in creating the category of 'the homosexual' in the late nineteenth century (see chapter 5). The categories of 'husband' and 'wife' are also partly constituted by state action, through mechanisms ranging from marriage laws to tax policy.

- Because of these activities and capacities, the state is the key target in gender politics. It is the focus of most political mobilization on gender issues (see chapter 8 below), as pressure groups and popular movements try to reach their goals via the state. Indeed, the rise of the liberal state was the focus of a historic change in the form of gender politics, which became mass politics for the first time in the nineteenth century. The demand for suffrage, 'votes for women', was precisely a demand to participate in decision-making within the state.
- Since gender relations are marked by crisis tendencies and structural change (chapter 4), the state as the heart of gendered power is itself liable to crisis and change. Current crisis tendencies which impinge on the state include problems of legitimation to do with men's violence, and tensions arising from the gender division of labour ('equal opportunity' and the 'glass ceiling' for women).

These conclusions were drawn from the first wave of feminist research on the state. This analysis had a certain solidity and realism. I think the points listed make a good first approximation to an understanding of the state and gender. But they also have limitations, which are easier to see now than they were ten years ago. Further issues have been emerging, especially to do with power, masculinity and globalization.

Theories of the state tend to forget that the state is only one of society's centres of power. A traditional definition of the state is the institution that holds a monopoly of the legitimate use of force in a given territory. But this is unrealistic. For instance, it ignores the domestic violence of husbands towards wives, a widespread social pattern which used to be wholly legitimate and whose legitimacy is only now being widely contested (Dobash and Dobash 1992).

Can we regard husbands as a 'power'? It flies in the face of conventional political analysis, but it makes sense. In a patriarchal gender order, husbands' interests in their wives' sexual and domestic services are institutionalized on a society-wide basis. This is a power to which state agencies have repeatedly accommodated. Wendy Hollway (1994) documents this point in a study of civil service employment practice in Tanzania. At the time, Tanzania had an official policy of equal conditions for men and women in public employment, as most countries now do. But this policy was subverted when it clashed with husbands' interests. For instance, women civil servants were sent on training programmes only if their husbands had given approval. 'Applications without a husband's permission were treated as if [official] permission had been withheld.' In other ways too, the claims of the state on its employees were modified when the employee was a wife.

Another kind of power is emerging in the form of 'security' agencies. There are said to be more private security employees in the United States now than there are publicly employed police. Corporations run surveillance programmes to control their own employees, and a significant branch of information technology helps them do this. Increasing numbers of the affluent live in 'gated communities', that is, housing complexes with fences patrolled by security employees, designed to keep out the poor, the black and the card-less.

These private security systems are gendered: controlled by men, mostly employing men, and in the case of the gated communities, en-gating women. Because their legitimacy depends on property, not citizenship, private security systems so far have escaped the political pressure for equal opportunity which women have been able to exert on the state.

The gendered state, then, is operating in a complex field of forces. Recognizing this helps explain the possibility of disintegration in state structures, as seen in the case of the Soviet Union discussed by Novikova (chapter 2). Seeing the gender side of this process may also help explain what many people have found baffling, the re-emergence of *ethnicity* as a basis of states – for instance, in the successor states to Yugoslavia in the Balkans.

Ethnicity is created, to a significant degree, through gender relations. The notion of extended kinship is central to the rhetoric of ethnic membership and boundaries: 'our kith and kin', as the British used to say; 'brothers born of warrior stock', in the language of Zulu nationalism in South Africa (Waetjen and Maré 2001). As Jill Vickers (1994) notes, ethnic politics lays heavy emphasis on women's reproductive powers. Gender relations thus provide a vehicle for both new claims to authority (all the leaders of warring ethnic successor states are men) and definitions of the boundaries of the group to which one feels loyal.

In discussions of politics 'gender' is often a code-word for 'women'. In this we are oddly like our Victorian great-grandfathers who spoke of women as 'the sex'. But it is essential to bring men and masculinity explicitly into the analysis of the state, as for any organization. Especially in an organization as large and complex as the state, it is important to recognize the distinction between hegemonic and subordinated masculinities (Messerschmidt 1993). The masculinization of the state, accurately identified in feminist theory, is principally a relationship between state institutions and hegemonic masculinity.

This relationship is a two-way street. State power is a resource for the struggle for hegemony in gender, and hegemonic masculinity is a resource in the struggle for state power. This is why political parties often run military heroes or prominent generals as candidates. Notable examples include President Dwight Eisenhower, the senior American general of the Second World War; his successor, President John Kennedy, a decorated front-line naval officer of the Second World War; and his opponent, Chancellor Adolf Hitler, a decorated front-line infantryman of the First World War.

Equally we need to acknowledge the complexity of women's relationships with the state. Julia O'Connor, Ann Orloff and Sheila Shaver in *States, Markets, Families* (1999) have recently published a sophisticated analysis of gender and welfare policy in four industrialized countries. They confirm how apparently gender-neutral policies actually have gender effects. For instance, retirement income systems may make better provision for people who have a continuous employment career (who happen to be mostly men) than for people who have done a lot of unpaid domestic work (mostly women). It is clear that the women's movement has been a force in welfare debates but its influence has been uneven. Different areas of state policy may show different gender patterns. The United States, for instance, has relatively poor income security for women, but relatively strong legal support for women's 'body rights'.

Differences among women are often important in gender policies beyond the welfare sector. Pro-natalist policies which encourage women to be mothers have often been race- and class-specific. The same state may attempt to prevent ethnic minority women from having babies, or regard them as pathological ('welfare queens') when they do. State agencies may discriminate against lesbians (e.g. in employment) in favour of heterosexual women, thus in broad terms helping sustain women's sexual availability to men. But they also provide pensions for women with dependent children under conditions that deny their sexual availability to men.

O'Connor, Orloff and Shaver's study shows clearly for gender issues that what is true of one state is not necessarily true of another, nor of the same state at another point of time. We need to speak of 'states', not just 'the state'. In the contemporary world some of the most important differences reflect the legacy of empire and the global inequalities of wealth.

The struggle to end the colonial empires necessarily challenged the gender arrangements of colonial societies. Some nationalist, revolutionary and anti-colonial movements mobilized women's support and contested traditional forms of patriarchy. The Chinese communist movement is the best-known case. The Maoist slogan 'women hold up half the sky' was part of a sustained attack on feudal attitudes and laws which had enforced the subordination of women (Stacey 1983). In many other places too, breaking down patriarchy and bringing women into the labour force was seen as vital for development.

But establishing a post-colonial or post-revolutionary regime has often meant installing a new version of patriarchy. Women have been brought into the labour force, but not equally into the political leadership. Maria Mies (1986) sardonically observes how post-colonial regimes symbolized the new patriarchy with cults of revolutionary Founding Fathers – including Mao. In some cases the exclusion of women is explicit: the intimidation of women by Islamic-revival movements in Afghanistan, Iran and some Arab countries is a current example. Nayereh Tohidi's (1991) narrative of feminist politics in Iran shows how assertive attitudes among women were seen as evidence of the corruption of religion and culture by Western influences. Most post-colonial states have been dependent on multinational corporations for their trade, investment and development, so – given the gendered character of large corporations, discussed in the last section – have been operating in an economic environment dominated by men. Singapore, one of the striking success stories of dependent capitalist development, has also created one of the most monolithic patriarchies in post-colonial government.

Yet the current is not all one way. There is also a history of women's activism in Islamic societies, and in certain cases – Pakistan and Indonesia – women have become prominent political leaders. The post-colonial state in India has provided a political environment in which a strong feminist movement could develop. And it is striking that of the five successor states to the British Indian Empire, three have had women Prime Ministers and a fourth nearly did. One of these was the first elected woman head of government in the world: Sirimavo Bandaranaike, elected Prime Minister of Sri Lanka in 1960.

In the countries which were once the imperial centres and are now the financial centres of the global economy, the massive accumulation of wealth has changed the conditions of gender politics. It allows, for instance, the rising lifespan and the 'demographic revolution' (drastic drop in birthrate) that has transformed the lives of married women in rich countries. The politics of reproduction take a specific shape in such circumstances: in these countries, the women's movement has struggled in courts and parliaments for rights to contraception and abortion. The famous court case 'Roe v. Wade', which established abortion rights in the USA, is regarded there as a key feminist victory.

The feminist movements which have been active in these countries since the nineteenth century have had a series of legal and constitutional victories, establishing broadly equal formal rights between women and men: the right to vote, the right to own property, the right to take legal action, fair employment practices, and so on. The old form of state patriarchy, with masculine authority embedded in bureaucratic hierarchies, was vulnerable to feminist challenge.

But the state has been changing. New agendas of 'reform' by right-wing governments have privatized many state services, and in other ways have made public services operate more like corporations. As the Australian sociologist Anna Yeatman (1990) points out, there has been a reorganization of state power in forms less open to feminist challenge. Indeed, women's increased presence in the public realm is counter-balanced by a decline of the public realm itself. Neo-liberal economic strategies, deregulating markets, reducing taxes and government services, and transferring resources to private businesses have meant a major relocation of power into corporations and market mechanisms dominated by men.

A striking feature of twentieth-century political history is the growth of agencies that link territorial states without themselves having a territorial base. They include the International Labour Organization, the League of Nations, the United Nations and its various agencies, the World Bank, the International Monetary Fund, the Organization for Economic Co-operation and Development. The European Union, equally important, is a more traditional political form: a regional customs union which has partly evolved into a federal state.

These agencies, too, are gendered, and have gender effects. For the most part their gender regimes copy those of the states that gave rise to them. The international agencies have, however, a specific importance in gender politics: they are an important vehicle for the globalization of gender relations. As inter-governmental organizations, their explicit gender politics is usually cautious and diplomatic. Yet their shape as organizations, and the rules they operate by, convey gender meanings. Inter-governmental forums tend to emphasize a formal equality between participants.

This became significant in the United Nations Decade for Women, 1975–85, the most sustained effort on gender issues by international organizations. The major conferences marking the Decade became an arena for conflict over the global significance of Western feminism. As Chilla Bulbeck shows in *One World Women's Movement* (1988), there was fierce debate about whether the American model, an autonomous women's movement, was relevant to the needs of third-world women. Some saw this as a new form of cultural imperialism, which by creating antagonisms between women and men and emphasizing issues that divided them would undermine popular struggles against Western domination.

Gender in world society

Though most discussions of gender are 'local', as mentioned at the start of this chapter, there has always been a counter-current in gender theory. Women's Liberation produced a theory of patriarchy which, in its more sophisticated forms, had historical depth and worldwide reach (Reiter 1977). Socialist feminism turned the focus onto the history of imperialism, and the contemporary world economy, as sources of gender inequality (Mies 1986). The rise of Black feminism in the United States, and post-colonial feminism in other parts of the world, called attention to the global diversity in women's situations and outlooks (Mohanty 1991).

This current of theory was strongly reinforced by a practical development: the creation of international forums for discussing gender inequalities and the interests of women. International women's organizations have existed for most of the twentieth century, such as the pacifist Women's International League for Peace and Freedom. What we now call 'gender' issues have been debated in international forums since before the First World War (Lenz, Szypulski and Molsich 1996: 10–12). Nevertheless the United Nations Decade for Women made a remarkable change. In the Decade for Women, and in follow-ups since, a series of high-profile conferences created a global forum for feminist ideas and pressed issues about the situation of women onto the attention of member governments. More than that, the UNDW crystallized a policy agenda around women's interests that has been pursued in a range of international agencies. This has now been made permanent (so far as such things ever are) by the creation of a United Nations Division for the Advancement of Women.

I believe that these developments reflect an important reality in gender relations today. There are significant features of the gender order which cannot be understood locally, which *require* analysis on a global scale. This applies to all the structures of gender relations described in chapter 4:

• The economic relations between women and men, in a time where large percentages of national economies are owned by foreigners, large sections of industry are dependent on foreign trade, and major investment decisions are made by transnational corporations;

- The politics of gender, in a time when global competitiveness is pursued via state restructuring, neo-liberalism and privatization of public services, and when masculinized military, paramilitary and police institutions are coordinated internationally;
- Changing emotional relations and sexuality associated with population control, the HIV/AIDS pandemic, and international travel;
- The symbolism of gender, in a time when particular images of masculinity and femininity circulate on a vast scale in global media (e.g. fashion, 'celebrities', professional sports), while gender ideologies from different cultures are interwoven as a result of large-scale migration, intermarriage and interaction of cultures.

If we can think at all of world society, of social organization at a planetary level, then we must be capable of thinking about gender as a structure of world society. To take this view we need not assume that gender is everywhere the same, as early theories of patriarchy did assume. Indeed it seems much more likely, at present, that the links are often loose and the correspondences uneven. All we need to assume is that significant linkages do exist.

The links that constitute a global gender order seem to be of two basic types: interaction between gender orders, and new arenas.

Interaction between gender orders

Imperial conquest, neo-colonialism, and the current world systems of power, investment, trade and communication, have brought very diverse societies in contact with each other. The gender orders of those societies have consequently been brought into contact with each other.

This has often been a violent and disruptive process. Imperialism included an assault on those local gender arrangements which did not fit the colonizers' templates: missionaries, for instance, tried to stamp out the third-gender 'berdache' tradition in North America, and what they saw as women's promiscuity in Polynesia. Local gender arrangements have been disrupted or reshaped by slavery, indentured labour, migration and resettlement (well illustrated by Moodie's study of South African mining, in chapter 2). In the contemporary world, the institutions of masculine violence in different parts of the world are linked by an arms trade that amounted to at least $US 24 billion in 1997 (United Nations Development Programme 1999).

The gender practices reshaped by such means form new patterns which are, so to speak, the first level of a global gender order. They are local, but carry the impress of the forces that make a global society. They can, in themselves, be the focus of social struggle. An important example is the controversy in some Islamic countries around the influence of Western models of femininity, symbolized by the debate about women not wearing the veil.

New arenas

Imperialism and globalization have created institutions that operate on a world scale. These institutions all have internal gender regimes, and each gender regime has its gender dynamic – interests, gender politics, processes of change. World-spanning institutions thus create new arenas for gender formation and gender dynamics. The most important of these institutions seem to be:

Transnational and multinational corporations Corporations operating in global markets are now the largest business organizations on the planet. The biggest ones, in industries like oil, car manufacturing, computers and telecommunications, have resources amounting to hundreds of billions of dollars and employ hundreds of thousands of people. They typically have a strong gender division of labour, and (as discussed above) a strongly masculinized management culture.

The international state United Nations agencies, the European Union and a range of other international agencies and agreements now exist. They regulate gender issues globally (e.g. through development aid, education, human rights and labour conventions). They are also important because they themselves have multicultural gender regimes, probably more complex than those of transnational corporations. This is because, as Dorota Gierycz (1999) observes, they often have staffing rules that guarantee geographical diversity.

International media Multinational media corporations circulate film, video, music and news on a very large scale. There are also more decentralized media (post, telegraph, telephone, fax, the Internet, the Web) and their supporting industries. All contain gender arrangements and circulate gender meanings. The newer media and applications, such as Web-based marketing, have a rapidly growing global reach.

Global markets It is important to distinguish markets themselves from the individual corporations that operate in them. International markets – capital, commodity, service and labour markets – have an increasing 'reach' into local economies. They are often strongly gender-structured and are now (with the political triumph of neo-liberalism) very weakly regulated.

In these arenas we can detect the outlines of a world gender order. It is imperfectly linked up, and far from homogeneous, but is already an important presence. Its weight in our lives will undoubtedly grow.

It is clear that the world gender order is the scene of significant injustice and other toxic effects. Though data on a world scale are very imperfect, we can map some significant differences in the situations of women and men:

Material inequalities and exploitation Perhaps the most basic inequality, the inequality of wealth, is exceptionally difficult to map on a world scale. Journalistic reports on the world's largest private fortunes indicate that the great majority are controlled by men. For instance, the list of 'World's Richest' for 2000 published by the business magazine *Forbes* identified 306 billionaires on the international scene, just twelve of whom are women. There is more information about income. Women's earned incomes average 59 per cent of men's in industrialized countries, 63 per cent of men's in Eastern Europe and the CIS, and 48 per cent of men's in developing countries (1997 data) – an average of 56 per cent world-wide. Time-budget studies show women's contribution to total social labour is no less than, and may be greater than, that of men, in both developing and industrialized countries (United Nations Development Programme 1999).

Education and cultural access One measure of social investment in education is the adult literacy rate. Total world figures are not available, but in groups of countries women's adult literacy rates range from 65 per cent of men's (least developed countries) to about 100 per cent of men's (1997). The situation in basic education has markedly improved, with female primary school enrolment now running at 95 per cent of the male rate world-wide. In advanced levels of education, larger gender gaps persist in some parts of the world (United Nations Development Programme 1999).

Institutional power Men held 87 per cent of seats in national parliaments, world-wide, in 1999 (down from 89 per cent in 1991). In terms of executive power, women held 7 per cent of ministerial posts, world-wide, in 1996 (up from 3 per cent in 1987). In no country in the world do women hold a majority of the ministerial posts. In a significant number of countries women hold no ministerial posts at all. Men hold almost all senior military commands, most appellate judicial positions, and almost all senior police commands (Inter-Parliamentary Union 1999,

Gierycz 1999). Practically every one of the world's largest corporations operating in global markets is headed by men. Women are also scarce in the leadership of business associations. As Valdés and Gomáriz (1995: 176) remark for Latin America, 'Women's presence in those organizations is modest, and nonexistent at the highest levels of leadership in many cases.'

Recognition Men hold a large majority of positions of intellectual authority, as professors, and are heads of most international scientific bodies. Men hold most religious authority, as bishops, patriarchs, imams, head monks. In several of the world's major religions women are formally excluded from authority. In international mass media, women are generally constituted as objects of desire rather than as subjects of significant action, recognized for beauty or fashion more than for accomplishments, wisdom or knowledge. Pornographic representations of women are increasingly common in international media including the Internet.

These patterns are far from uniform. The statistics show diversity among countries and regions of the world which reflects their different histories, different background cultures, and different levels of social wealth. For instance, women were 39 per cent of members of national parliaments in the Nordic countries in 1999, 9 per cent in the Pacific countries and 4 per cent in Arab states. In recent decades the countries of Scandinavia have stood out as world leaders on such measures, reflecting the strength of the women's movement, a well established local welfare state and an egalitarian culture.

An important current development in gender studies is the attempt to map the international patterns of inequality. A notable example is the 'Mujeres Latinoamericanas en Cifras' project coordinated by the Facultad Latinoamericana de Ciencias Sociales (Valdés and Gomáriz 1995), a tremendous data compilation comparing the position of women and men in nineteen countries of Latin America. Among other things this project traced the feminization of poverty, the changing occupational structure, demographic change, education, etc.

Broadly, the evidence shows that men are the beneficiaries where gender inequalities exist. But not all men benefit to the same degree, indeed some men do not benefit at all. Many men pay some cost, and some pay a heavy cost, for the general supremacy of men in a patriarchal gender order.

Men are the vast majority of the world's 20 million military personnel. Not surprisingly, men are the majority of those killed and injured in combat (though the picture is different for the civilian victims of war). Men are also the majority of victims in reported homicide and assault. In industrialized countries, and in Eastern Europe and the CIS, men's suicides outnumber women's suicides by 3 to 1 and 5 to 1 respectively.

Because of the combination of higher labour force participation and the gender division of labour, men suffer higher rates of injury, including road transport injury. Across Latin America, for instance, men's rate of death by accident is three times higher than the rate for women (Valdés and Gomáriz 1995: 124). Men in most parts of the world have higher rates of smoking, alcohol use and narcotics use than women. For these among other reasons, men (except in certain very poor countries) have a lower average life expectancy than women. Certain groups of men, notably homosexual men and men of minority ethnic or religious groups, are targeted for abuse and sometimes violence.

Gender inequalities and toxicity are thus features of the global gender order, as well as national societies. Political struggles inevitably result. The patterns of world gender politics will be examined in chapter 8.

7

Gender and the Intellectuals

A century and a half ago there was no theory of gender in the modern sense. When in 1848 the women and men of the suffrage movement gathered at Seneca Falls in upstate New York for the now-famous convention that launched feminism as a political movement, they looked back to the moralists of the eighteenth century, rather than to the new social sciences around them, for their inspiration.

Then, the underlying problem in understanding gender was to create a framework. At the beginning of the twenty-first century, not only do we have a theory of gender, we have a library of them. Now, a major problem in understanding gender is to make sense of the multiple frameworks on offer.

In this chapter I will try to do this historically. To speak of 'theories of gender' abstractly is to imply that all the theories are about the same thing, that they have the same object of knowledge. This is, at best, only approximately correct. Theories do not appear out of thin air. They are created in varying historical circumstances, by people who have different backgrounds, different places in the social order, different training and different tools. History throws different problems at them. It is not surprising that they formulate their intellectual projects, and understand their object of knowledge, in differing ways.

This point is basic to the sociology of knowledge. It was first applied to gender by a student of the sociology of knowledge, Viola Klein, in her forgotten classic *The Feminine Character: History of an Ideology* (1946). In a later generation it was re-emphasized by feminist 'standpoint epistemology', such as Sandra Harding's *The Science Question in Feminism*

(1986), a book which explored the interplay between gender relations and the construction of scientific knowledge.

To understand the history of ideas about gender, then, it is necessary to study the intellectuals who produced them, and the broad cultural perspectives within which gender issues, at different times, arose. I will try to do this by tracing the circumstances in which four main waves of Western gender theory were produced, considering in each case the problems facing a generation of intellectuals, and the changing ways in which knowledge was constituted in response.

This account is specifically about Western gender theories. As I have noted in earlier chapters, other cultures also have ways of talking about, or accounting for, gender issues. But these accounts do not generally take the form of empirical research or descriptive and analytic theory. Those genres, as a way of understanding human relations, developed in the distinctive context of the Western human sciences.

Science, suffrage and empire (c.1860–1920)

Western gender theories are products of a secular, rationalist and sceptical culture which took its modern shape, so far as the human sciences are concerned, in the second half of the nineteenth century. The human sciences were mainly produced by intellectuals of the great imperial powers, in Europe and North America – though their ideas fairly rapidly circulated in other parts of the world, from Chile to Japan.

Gender theories came into existence by the gradual transformation of older discourses of gender which were religious, non-rational and moralistic. Early feminist statements like Mary Wollstonecraft's *Vindication of the Rights of Women* (1792), produced in immediate response to the celebration of the 'Rights of Man' in the French Revolution, were still mainly embedded in a discourse of moral improvement. The frame of reference was more religious than scientific. Similarly, the early suffrage movement in the United States was in large part a religious movement. The Seneca Falls convention borrowed the moralizing language of the Declaration of Independence for its message.

Already, however, religion was being displaced by science as the major frame of intellectual life. Nineteenth-century science, for the most part the creation of men of bourgeois background, was actively concerned with problems that related to gender. This involved Charles Darwin himself, the towering figure in evolutionary thought. *The Origin of Species* (1859) made inheritance and biological selection into first-rank intellectual issues. Darwin's later work specifically addressed the choice of sexual partners and the evolutionary role of sex as a form of reproduction.

This occurred in a time and place when the gender division of labour, and symbolic divisions between women and men, were at an extreme. The 'separate spheres' of men and women were powerfully emphasized in mid-Victorian bourgeois culture. It is not surprising that in this milieu evolutionary thought – 'Darwinism' more than Darwin – produced the idea of a biological basis for gender difference, which has been so influential ever since (see chapter 3 above).

Even before social Darwinism became influential, gender issues ran through early attempts to formulate a science of society. The French philosopher Auguste Comte, the founder of positivism and a figure almost as influential as Darwin, gave close attention to the social function of women in the first 'treatise of sociology', his *System of Positive Polity* (1851). Women were, in his view, an important social base for the coming utopian society – but only if they remained in their proper sphere as comforters and nurturers of men. It was over this issue that Comte and his most distinguished follower, the British philosopher John Stuart Mill, parted company. Mill later published a famous essay, *The Subjection of Women* (1869), arguing the case for equality.

Though it is now largely forgotten, the men of the metropolitan intelligentsia who worked to create modern social science paid as much attention to gender issues as to any others. When Lester Ward wrote the first major theoretical statement in American sociology, *Dynamic Sociology* (1883), he offered a long analysis of the 'reproductive forces' with a detailed critique of 'sexuo-social inequalities' such as unequal education for girls and boys. In 1879 the German labour leader August Bebel published a book, *Woman and Socialism*, which became a best-seller. Marx's colleague Friedrich Engels wrote a long essay, *The Origin of the Family, Private Property and the State* (1884) which drew on academic debates about the history of the family and the idea of 'matriarchy', as well as socialists' concerns about 'the woman question' as an issue of social reform.

Why did the men, who as beneficiaries of a patriarchal system had an interest in *not* raising questions about it, take this interest? To a significant extent, because of pressure from the women in their milieu – as Lester Ward acknowledged. 'The woman question' was placed on the agenda by an emerging movement of women, which was particularly strong in exactly those social groups from which the new social scientists came. The issue of the 'subjection of women' was unavoidable for middle-class intellectuals trying to formulate (as all social science at the time did) theories of social progress. The suffrage movement, and writers like Wollstonecraft and Mill, had made the emancipation of women a test of the 'progress' achieved by any society.

Women intellectuals in these generations were operating under such difficulties that they were unlikely to produce theoretical treatises themselves. (Among other things, women were then excluded from almost all universities.) One hardly finds a 'theory of gender' in the writings of feminist intellectuals such as Harriet Martineau in Britain, Susan B. Anthony in the United States, or Maybanke Wolstenholme in Australia – though one finds many insights into the mechanisms of patriarchy. Their attention was more focused on the critique of prejudice among men, or on practical problems of organizing for the suffrage, law reform, and education for women.

When more theoretical writing by women developed, in texts such as Olive Schreiner's *Woman and Labour* (1911), it was closely connected with employment issues. Schreiner analysed the 'parasitism' of bourgeois women and the refusal of bourgeois society to recognize its exploitation of working women. Parasitism could be broken by opening all spheres of work to women: 'We claim, today, all labour for our province!'

By the turn of the twentieth century there was a world-wide labour and socialist movement which had its own intelligentsia, and which provided – most notably in Germany, but to some extent around the capitalist world – an organizational base for radical women. A sharp controversy developed about the extent to which working-class and bourgeois women had shared interests. For instance Alexandra Kollontai's *The Social Basis of the Woman Question* (1909) argued vehemently that there was no general 'women's question', and that support by working-class women for socialism was the only path towards true equality. This did not prevent Kollontai arguing for separate organization of women within the labour movement, and also pioneering debates about sexual freedom and the reform of marriage.

One other experience decisively shaped theories about gender: the experience of empire. The intellectuals of Paris, London, Petersburg and New York were living in the heartlands of the greatest wave of imperial expansion the world has ever known. During the nineteenth century direct conquest (as in Africa, India, North America and Australasia), and economic domination (as in South America and China) brought an unprecedented range of cultures into the European orbit. The gender orders of these societies often differed drastically from the conquerors'.

Though the conquerors were in no doubt about whose gender arrangements were better – their own were plainly justified by the Law of Progress – they had to take note of diversity. Explorers, conquerors, missionaries and curious travellers gathered an immense fund of information about gender arrangements in the non-European world, which they often thought were survivals from the primitive days of mankind. Texts such as Engels's *Origin* testify to the fascination of this information for metropolitan intellectuals. Early social anthropology is full of it. The monuments of armchair anthropology, such as J. G. Frazer's genial and encyclopaedic masterpiece *The Golden Bough* (1890), blend lore from the imperial frontier with classical literature and European folklore.

Beyond this scholarly work, the popular imperialism of the late nineteenth and early twentieth centuries put many exotic images of gender into circulation: polygamy, marriage by conquest, concubinage, amazon women, primitive promiscuity, and so on. A serious comparative science of gender was slow to emerge; it first appeared in the anthropological theory of kinship systems. Nevertheless, by the beginning of the twentieth century the news from the empire was already acting alongside feminism to destabilize belief in a fixed gender order.

The gender theories that appeared in this period were strongly categorical, based on a taken-for-granted dichotomy of men and women. This is not surprising given the 'separate spheres' in the social groups from which most of the theorists came. For all their interest in exotic gender customs, European intellectuals took little notice of the trickle of news from the frontier about exotic gender *forms* such as 'third genders'. Their thinking about gender relations focused mainly on personal interaction, the most easily grasped level of analysis. Thus Mill, trying to explain the subjection of women, could not find a better explanation than men's physical force. However, there was increasing attention to social structure as the socialist economic argument kicked in. Already gender debates were dealing with a range of issues that we can recognize in modern gender research: power ('subjection'), sexuality ('phylogenetic forces', 'free love'), and the division of labour ('parasitism').

However modern the issues look, the way they were interpreted was very different from approaches a hundred years later. To the Victorian intelligentsia the main determinant of gender patterns was the dynamic of 'progress', loosely linked with biology in evolutionary speculation but to all intents and purposes an autonomous social process. From Mill to Schreiner it was progress – moral, economic and political – that was thought to be breaking the bonds of ancient custom and lifting gender relations onto a higher and more rational plane. In almost all theorizing about gender in these generations, this was the frame. Gender issues arose within this frame, as a dimension or problem of progress. The idea of a 'theory of gender' as an intellectual undertaking in its own right was alien to this whole way of thought.

Psychoanalysis and reaction (c.1920–1965)

If the keynote of the first period was the connection of gender with the sciences of progress, the keynote of the second was the decoding or deconstruction of gender accomplished by the new depth psychology.

Psychoanalysis was at the start a medical innovation, a form of therapy. When the Viennese nerve specialist Sigmund Freud became convinced that many of his patients' troubles were psychological not physical in origin, he explored their emotional lives for causes, and developed new interpretive methods to do so. His patients' talk, during long courses of therapy, gave him masses of evidence about the troubled emotional interior of the bourgeois family. This case-history material he worked up in two ways. One was psychological biography of individual patients, illustrating Freud's method and giving concrete examples of his new concepts. The most famous are 'Dora' (1905) and the 'Wolf Man' (1918). The second was theoretical work where he set out, and over several decades revised, his new depth psychology. The most important of these writings expounded the concepts of unconscious motivation (*The Interpretation of Dreams*, 1900), childhood sexuality, the oedipus complex and the transformations of desire and attachment in the course of growing up (*Three Essays on the Theory of Sexuality*, 1905), and the connections between depth psychology and culture (*Civilization and its Discontents*, 1930).

There has been endless critique and revision of these ideas, and of others which Freud offered in the course of a long and productive life. Psychoanalysis developed into a kind of scientific and therapeutic cult, which soon split and became multiple cults. Medicine and academic psychology picked up some of its ideas and denounced others. Even the concept of the unconscious remains controversial in psychology a hundred years later. But by the 1920s Freud's ideas had spread far beyond their original technical audience and had become a cultural force. It was clear that, whether right or wrong in the fine detail, Freud had put his finger on problems which were both troubling and important for

modern Western societies. He laid bare, we might say, key crisis tendencies in the structure of emotional relationships.

Freud's sharp insight into bourgeois society, it is often suggested,
stemmed from his slightly marginal position as a Jewish professional man
in a world of growing anti-Semitism. There was a wider avant-garde
culture in Vienna at the time, including a suffrage movement. Freud was
not directly a supporter of the women's movement, but doubtless he was
influenced by contemporary feminism in the problems he addressed. His
first major follower, Alfred Adler, was also Jewish, had close links to
the social-democratic labour movement, and did explicitly support
feminism. As I mentioned in chapter 5, Adler (1927) made the critique
of masculinity a centrepiece of his revision of psychoanalysis.

These two pioneers, and the next generation of psychoanalysts who
debated sexuality, femininity and masculinity in the 1920s and early
1930s, showed between them that the gender divisions of adulthood
were not fixed from the start of life. Rather, the adult patterns were
constructed in a conflict-ridden process of development over the life-
course. This was a decisive shift in ideas about gender. Nineteenth-century
thought, even feminism, had taken the fixed characters of men and women
more or less for granted.

Though Freud's and Adler's ideas were formulated at the high tide of
first-wave feminism, the influence of psychoanalysis spread when feminism was in retreat, after the Great War. From the 1920s to the 1960s
radical politics and avant-garde culture in Europe and North America
was controlled by men, in movements which had no use for feminism
or sexual liberation, nor for their advocates. This was especially true of
economistic socialism, which in two forms – the militant bureaucracy
which eventually called itself the 'communist party', and the trade union
confederations and parliamentary labour parties which called themselves
'democratic socialists' – dominated left-wing politics in this generation.

Witness the fate of Alexandra Kollontai, who was an important
Bolshevik leader in the revolutionary period. Under Stalin's dictatorship
she was pushed aside into minor diplomatic posts, and was lucky to
escape execution. Or witness the fate of Wilhelm Reich, the most brilliant social thinker among psychoanalysts. He was expelled from both
the psychoanalytic movement and the communist movement, and wound
up as the leader of a tiny, crazy cult of his own.

These decades saw the vote gained by women in most of the metropolitan powers. They also saw the rise of fascism, which wiped out
feminism and psychoanalysis in Central Europe. The war against fascism
was followed by the McCarthyite reaction in the West, which regarded

feminists and homosexuals as agents of communist subversion. The communists, for their part, regarded feminists and homosexuals as symptoms of capitalist decadence. (Having survived Hitler and Stalin, Reich was finally arrested in the 1950s by the US government, and died in gaol.)

Some new forms of women's activism emerged, such as the birth control movement. Marie Stopes's influential *Married Love* appeared in 1918. This activism gave rise to little in the realm of ideas. In more abstract forms, interrogation of the categories of gender continued, and began to move towards a more explicit theory of gender.

The landmark is Mathilde Vaerting's *The Dominant Sex*, first published in 1921. Vaerting, a reforming educator, was one of the first two women to be appointed to a professorial chair in a German university. She met with an extremely hostile reaction, was thrown out of her job when Hitler came to power, and never held a university chair again. Understandably, she had a lifelong interest in the sociology of power.

The Dominant Sex criticized the notion of a fixed masculine and feminine character on sociological grounds. Basing herself shakily on a speculative history of ancient Egypt and Sparta, and more firmly on an environmental view of character, Vaerting argued that masculinity and femininity basically reflected power relations. In societies where women held power, she argued, men showed the very characteristics which bourgeois society saw as quintessentially feminine. In developing this argument, Vaerting created what might be seen as the first extended theory of gender. Her argument linked psychological patterns with social structure, and distinguished law, the division of labour, and ideology as spheres of gender domination. She even offered an amazing prediction of Men's Liberation as a sequel of feminism. But the empirical base of her argument was shaky, and in the European upheavals of the mid-twentieth century her work faded into obscurity.

A more impressive empirical base for gender theory was taking shape about the same time in social anthropology, with its newly developed technique of field study, 'ethnography'. The best-known ethnographers, from the Polish Bronisław Malinowski to the American Margaret Mead, paid close attention to sex and gender. Malinowski's pioneering ethnography in the Trobriand Islands (off New Guinea) offered detailed descriptions of sexuality, marriage and divisions of labour. In *Sex and Repression in Savage Society* (1927) Malinowski used this information in a famous critique of psychoanalysis, arguing that the 'oedipus complex' as described by Freud was not universal. Different patterns of emotional development flow from different kinship structures, such as matrilineal kinship.

Mead's early research in Samoa reinforced the idea of cultural diversity in sexual conduct. Then in a widely read book called *Sex and Temperament in Three Primitive Societies* (1935) Mead exploded the idea of a fixed relationship between biological sex and gendered character. In her fieldwork in New Guinea, as she describes it herself,

> I found three tribes all conveniently within a hundred mile area. In one, both men and women act as we expect women to act – in a mild parental responsive way; in the second, both act as we expect men to act – in a fierce initiating fashion; and in the third, the men act according to our stereotype for women – are catty, wear curls and go shopping, while the women are energetic, managerial, unadorned partners.

These studies, with a growing library of other ethnographies, relativized the picture of gender. They gave credible and often sympathetic portraits of non-Western societies where gender arrangements functioned perfectly well, though along quite different lines from bourgeois life in the metropole.

Awareness of the relativity of gender helped to popularize the concept of 'sex roles' in the 1940s and 1950s. The concept of 'social role', formulated in anthropology, rapidly spread into sociology and psychology. The term became especially popular in the United States at a time when this country was becoming dominant in world social science. The idea of a male and a female sex role was a simple application of the general notion that people's social conduct reflects conformity to cultural norms for the social positions they occupy.

The most influential formulation of sex role theory was made by the most influential sociological theorist of the era, the Harvard University professor Talcott Parsons. In *Family Socialization and Interaction Process* (Parsons and Bales 1956), he proposed the most radically sociological theory of gender since Vaerting's, pushing beyond Malinowski's and Mead's positions which had always assumed some biological determination.

Parsons treated the distinction between male and female role as a difference of social function. His much-quoted characterization of the male role as 'instrumental' and the female role as 'expressive' defined a polarity that arises, Parsons thought, through the dynamics of social groups as such. Other writers about sex roles simply parked the instrumental/expressive distinction on top of biological difference, and presumed that the role norms expressed or elaborated the natural difference. Parsons was more rigorous. He wove Freudian ideas about child development into his account of socialization into the role norms. But he still treated the whole gender process as a consequence of the social system's need for integration and stability.

The popularity of what amounted to a theory of social conformity – role theory – among American academics in the repressive 1950s is not surprising. Yet it is worth noting that sex role theory in this generation, in the hands of Parsons and even more in the hands of academic women, was concerned also with *changes* in sex roles.

This discussion was initially about American women, who had seen spectacular changes in the gender division of labour during the Second World War, as well as longer-term changes in sexual practice and ideology. So Mirra Komarovsky (who many years later became president of the American Sociological Association, the second woman ever elected to that position) had good reason to theorize 'Cultural contradictions and sex roles', the title of a 1946 paper. In 1964 Komarowsky published *Blue Collar Marriage*, a sad though observant study of working-class wives under economic change and political reaction. Sex role change was also possible for men. Helen Hacker suggested this in a pioneering paper, 'The new burdens of masculinity' (1957). In consumer capitalism and suburban life, she argued, expressive functions were being added to instrumental, so that men were now expected to show interpersonal skills as well as being 'sturdy oaks'.

There was a feminist colouring in some sex role discussions, including Hacker's. But the renewal of feminist gender theory in the mid-century was basically the work of Simone de Beauvoir in France. *The Second Sex* (1949) drew on psychoanalysis, literature, and the activist philosophy worked out by de Beauvoir's partner Jean-Paul Sartre, to challenge gender categories and gender domination at the same time.

Refusing to take the polarity of masculine and feminine for granted, de Beauvoir explored how women were constituted as 'other' in the consciousness of men. She went on, in a remarkable series of social portraits, to explore the variety of ways in which women could respond to this situation and constitute themselves – not escaping from gender, for that was impossible, but realizing gender differently in different life projects. This work, too, was stimulated by the upheaval of war, and de Beauvoir's topics overlapped substantially with those of sex role research. But what she could see in these topics was different, because her approach stemmed from a political critique of the subordination of women.

By the mid-century this was exceptional. The subversive possibilities in deconstructive gender theory had mostly been tamed. Psychoanalysis had for the most part become a socially conservative branch of medicine, much more concerned to normalize people than to pursue an agenda of liberation. A measure of this trend was the reversal of psychoanalytic ideas about homosexuality. Freud had refused to regard homosexuality as pathological, but by the 1950s orthodox psychoanalysis had defined homosexuality as mental illness. Sex role theory was also, in the main, a conservative approach – especially as it was applied in counselling, social work, and schools. Simone de Beauvoir's cutting edge found many admirers, but no immediate popular response. *The Second Sex* was, symbolically, presented to English-speaking readers in 1953 with a condescending preface by a male academic translator.

The moment of Women's Liberation (*c.*1965–1980)

It was this intellectual situation in the mid-century, as well as the energy from young women in the radical social movements of the 1960s, that gave an explosive quality to the Women's Liberation movement – and guaranteed it would have a lasting impact.

Women's Liberation was mainly a movement of young intellectuals in Western cities. They came from an intelligentsia that had undergone great change since the beginning of the century. The growing economic and military importance of organized knowledge (indicated by new technologies such as atomic power and computers) coincided with, and partly drove, a huge expansion of secondary schools and university systems. A new generation of students and teachers were radicalized by the US civil rights movement, the Vietnam War, and struggles against the post-war capitalist oligarchies of Europe. The dramatic victories of anti-colonialist movements over two decades from 1945 seemed to prove that the world could change, that even massive power structures were vulnerable. The women of this intelligentsia provided an unprecedented base for feminist mobilization and theory, a potential that was, for many, triggered by their experience of discrimination at the hands of men in the radical movements themselves.

An extraordinarily rapid mobilization occurred in the late 1960s and early 1970s, across much of the advanced capitalist world. This movement produced a categorical approach to gender, emphasizing the solidarity of women as an oppressed group or a 'sex class' – which ran counter to the deconstructive trend of earlier gender theory. US feminism especially was sweepingly hostile to psychoanalysis, responding to the conservative force it had become.

The characteristic Women's Liberation position was based on a categorical theory of power. The term 'patriarchy' was retrieved from an anthropological backwater and used to name systems of male power. It was not expected that men would reform a system that privileged them. Patriarchy had to be confronted by an autonomous women's movement, and the demand for the liberation of women was a revolutionary demand. This view was expounded in a torrent of pamphlets and a series of vivid books, from Shulamith Firestone's *Dialectic of Sex* (1971) to Robin Morgan's famous anthology *Sisterhood is Powerful* (1970) and Sheila Rowbotham's *Women's Liberation and the New Politics* (1969). Even men influenced by the new feminism began to speak this language. Calls for 'male liberation', in solidarity with women's liberation rather than against it, soon appeared (Sawyer 1970).

In the feminism of the late 1960s it was usually assumed that a radical position on gender was part of a general social radicalism, which fought against gender, class and racial oppression at the same time. The radical movements of the day shared a belief that these systems could and would be overthrown. This perspective was immediately shared by the first theorists of Gay Liberation, who added sexual oppression to the agenda in texts such as Dennis Altman's *Homosexual: Oppression and Liberation* (1972) and Guy Hocquenghem's *Homosexual Desire* (1972).

By the mid-1970s, however, a gender-specific view had come to prominence in the United States and Britain. This view sharply separated gender struggles from others, or saw the oppression of women as the root of all social inequality. This version of categorical power theory came to be called 'radical feminism', 'revolutionary feminism', or, with a different emphasis, 'cultural feminism'. It responded to, and also partly contributed to, the breakup of the coalition that had driven radical politics in the 1960s and early 1970s.

This perspective was dramatically presented by the American theologian Mary Daly in *Gyn/Ecology* (1978). Daly tried to create a new conceptual and expressive language to express women's consciousness and women's anger against men, as part of an effort to create a distinct women's culture expressing the common interests of women. Increasingly, the social radicalism of early Women's Liberation was defined as an alternative, and impure, variant of feminism – 'socialist feminism' or 'marxist feminism'. By the 1980s this shift had gone so far that Catharine MacKinnon could claim the pure line of descent for radical feminism simply by calling it Feminism Unmodified.

The impulse of Women's Liberation was so powerful, however, that it launched a number of other theoretical movements beside this one. A categorical theory that focused on the division of labour, emphasizing the economic exploitation of women within the family, was proposed in a famous essay 'The main enemy' by Christine Delphy (1984) in France. Political economy, or radical economics, was brought into play to analyse women's exploitation. A complex debate ran through the 1970s on how to theorize women's domestic labour, and whether capitalists or husbands were the main beneficiaries of women's work (Malos 1980).

The familiar 'sex role' concept was radicalized. This was now treated as an account of the social controls that hampered women. Role norms once seen as woman's sacred duty – from putting-pink-booties-on-the-baby to getting-coffee-for-the-boss – were now described with contempt. The idea that gender consisted of social norms and expectations became an agenda for action, as it was assumed that the norms could be changed by concerted effort. In the United States there was a wave of enthusiasm for the attempt by the psychologist Sandra Bem (1974) to define and measure 'androgyny' as a goal of sex role reform. A debate about the 'male sex role' and how men could break out of it, or at least bend it, began in the United States and spilled into several other countries (e.g. Pleck and Sawyer 1974).

Other feminists, especially those from a socialist background, began to use the techniques of structuralism, the most influential intellectual movement in the human sciences at the time. In 1975, in a long essay called 'The traffic in women: notes on the "political economy" of sex', Gayle Rubin integrated feminism and anthropology in a sophisticated general theory of 'the sex/gender system'. This was perhaps the most ambitious theory of gender since Vaerting's. However, it was not isolated. A structural account of women's subordination had been proposed as early as 1966 by Juliet Mitchell in an essay, 'Women: the longest revolution', in the British *New Left Review*. In 1974, in *Psychoanalysis and Feminism*, Mitchell drew on structural anthropology and structuralist interpretations of Freud to account for the reproduction of patriarchy over time.

Mitchell's book, along with the work of Nancy Chodorow (1978) and others in the United States, marked a striking reversal of the feminist coolness towards psychoanalysis in the English-speaking world. The power of Freudian concepts to explain people's acceptance of oppressive social relations was again recognized. In France the rejection of psychoanalysis had not been so marked, as Simone de Beauvoir's work shows. In the wake of Women's Liberation, adaptations of Lacan's psychoanalysis were undertaken by a group of women, not all of whom called themselves feminists. The attempt was made, in a variety of ways, to find a level of human reality which escaped the phallocentric ordering of ordinary language and consciousness. Julia Kristeva's *Revolution in Poetic Language* (1974) and Luce Irigaray's essay *This Sex which is not One* (1977) were perhaps the most influential in this project.

It was, however, a simpler feminist adaptation of psychoanalysis and developmental psychology, Carol Gilligan's *In a Different Voice* (1982), that captured popular attention in the English-speaking world and became a best-seller. This was a return to categorical theory at the level of 'voice'. It was widely read as proving that men and women had different moral senses, and this reception was a portent of the sweeping popularity of simplified Jungian models of male/female difference that was to come in the 1990s.

The age of diversity (*c.*1980–2000)

By the late 1970s the political context of debates about gender was already changing in the rich countries. Feminism was winning a significant degree of institutional power. Feminism entered the state bureaucracy with equal opportunity and other programmes. The women administering these programmes, and giving policy advice to governments on women's issues, emerged as an important voice in feminism. They were called 'femocrats' in Australia where they were particularly influential: their story is vividly told in Hester Eisenstein's *Inside Agitators* (1996). Simultaneously feminism became established in universities.

The movement of feminists into government – to run programmes such as shelters for battered women, women's health centres, equal employment opportunity programmes, and school initiatives for girls – created sharp debate, given the Women's Liberation view of the state as part of the patriarchal system. But these programmes rapidly took hold in favourable political conditions, especially where there were labour or social-democratic governments, in Scandinavia, Canada, Australia and (at regional level) Germany. The work of the 'femocrats' posed new intellectual questions: how to understand the gender dynamics of the organizations in which feminists now found themselves, as well as how to understand the policy problems which the programmes addressed.

Accordingly several new branches of theory and research developed. From tentative beginnings in the 1970s a feminist organization theory emerged: sociologists such as Joan Acker in the United States and Peta Tancred in Canada (Mills and Tancred 1992) analysed the gender regimes of bureaucracies and corporations. The early view of the state as a direct expression of male power was reconsidered. In the 1980s a number of theorists began to examine the state as a gendered institution of great complexity, with significant possibilities of internal change (see chapter 6). Research institutes and monitoring programmes were set up, such as the Norwegian Likestillingssenteret (Centre for Gender Equality). A whole genre of feminist or feminist-inspired policy studies began to appear. To take just one field, education: notable policy studies range from the pioneering Australian report *Girls, School and Society* (1975) sponsored by the national Schools Commission, to the American Association of University Women's *How Schools Shortchange Girls* (1992), to the recent and very sophisticated British study *Closing the Gender Gap* by Madeleine Arnot and her colleagues (1999).

In the academic world the 1970s and 1980s saw a huge growth of feminist or feminist-inspired research in almost every discipline of the humanities and social sciences, and to a lesser extent in the natural sciences. In sociology, for instance, sex and gender – formerly a marginal field of low prestige – became the most active field of research in the whole discipline. Journals publishing research about sex roles, gender, women, and eventually men, multiplied. Some of them, including *Signs*, a US feminist journal launched in 1975, became high-prestige mainstream academic journals. By the 1980s 'women's studies' had emerged as an academic field in its own right.

At one level this was a startling success for feminism. The patriarchal monologue in universities was interrupted almost at once. As feminist academics moved up the promotion ladder, research funds flowed and Women's Studies programmes consolidated, a new social base for feminist thought had been established. Yet Women's Liberation movement activists looked on the early stages of this triumph with distrust, fearing that academic feminism would lose its political urgency, separate itself from grassroots campaigns, and become unintelligible to working women.

Everything that the activists feared has happened. Academic feminism has had to operate in academic modes, to share in the bureaucratic and cultural processes of universities. Women, like men, can become more concerned with their own careers than with other women's needs. Not all have done so; many academic women remain dedicated to reform. But the internal pressures of the institution are formidable, and the 'ivory tower' insulation does work. Part of academic feminism has pursued intellectual agendas that are only remotely connected with gender reform.

So, while one network of feminist researchers produces policy studies, another network has generated an abstract literature of high theory. Its main points of reference are intellectual developments among philosophers, literary and social theorists working on problems remote from gender.

The most prominent of these influences have been Michel Foucault and Jacques Derrida in France. The feminist application of Foucault's studies of discourse, micro-politics, and the regulation of bodies, has been discussed in earlier chapters. Derrida's influence has been more indirect, though he has had a technical impact on feminist philosophy. More widely, his argument on the indefinite deferral of meaning in language, and his development of the technique of deconstruction, have been taken as warrant for questioning the stability of all concepts and all identities – including the categories on which feminist thought rested.

A book pursuing this theme, Judith Butler's *Gender Trouble* (1990), became the most influential text in academic feminism in the 1990s. Butler argued that there are no fixed foundations of gender categories and therefore of feminist strategy. Gender is performative, bringing identities into existence through action, rather than expressive of some pre-existing reality. In Butler's treatment, gender radicalism consists, not of mobilization around an identity (such as 'women'), but of actions that subvert identity, disrupt gender dichotomy and displace gender norms.

The growth of cultural studies, a genre of commentary on mass culture and ideology in industrial and post-industrial society, has also strongly influenced women's studies. A rich literature of cultural analysis of gender has grown up (see chapters 4 and 5). But where feminists initially criticized media sexism with the expectation of changing the media, there is no such expectation in most current cultural analysis. A large part of gender theory has become contemplative or analytical in style, or rests content with small-scale subversions.

This shift in feminist theory is of course related to the broader cultural and political environment. In the late 1970s the 'new left' generally was fragmenting and Women's Liberation as a participatory social movement broke up. The movement became sharply divided over issues of sexuality (Segal 1994). Externally, feminism was running into stiffer resistance. A strong religious-right mobilization in the United States put a large effort into campaigns against abortion rights and sexual freedoms, and in favour of the 'traditional family'. A broader political reaction stopped the Equal Rights Amendment in the United States, and brought the Reagan, Thatcher and Kohl administrations to power, blocking feminist influence on national policy in the United States, Britain and Germany. In countries where centre-left governments were elected in the 1980s, including France and Australia, early openings towards feminism were squeezed by the influence of monetarism and neo-liberalism, and by the roll-back of social programmes under the pressure of global capital.

Open homophobia re-emerged in mainstream politics, particularly vicious around the HIV/AIDS epidemic. Anti-feminism and homophobia were themes in a growing fringe of racist and chauvinist groups, which gained particular strength in France and by 2000 had entered the political mainstream in Austria. In the United States the far right mounted a campaign of firebombings and assassinations against abortion providers.

There continued to be gains for gender reform. The most spectacular were in Scandinavia, where women arrived en masse in party politics and achieved an unprecedented level of representation in parliaments. In 1991, for instance, the leaders of all three major parties in Norway were women, including the Prime Minister Gro Harlem Brundtland. In the late 1990s the centrist governments of Clinton, Blair and Schröder provided renewed protection for a mild official feminism. But the political alternative, over most of the capitalist world, was a hard neo-liberalism, exalting the market and attacking what remained of the welfare state. Right-wing governments such as the Howard government in Australia removed funding from women's programmes which had any oppositional character, dispersed the femocrats and abandoned public commitments to gender reform.

This course of events has provoked many re-examinations of feminism and theories of gender. One such move was led by Black feminists in North America, who argued that uncritical use of the category 'women' in radical and liberal feminism concealed the realities of racism. There were not only differences of experience and identity between white and coloured women, but actual relations of exclusion or exploitation – for instance the presence of low-paid Black or Latina domestic workers in the households of white professional women. For some American Black feminists, including bell hooks (1984), that argument led back to the inclusive radicalism of early Women's Liberation and a renewed concern with integrating class, race and gender struggles. But in the changed circumstances of the 1980s and 1990s there was not a popular radicalism to support that response. The emphasis on race and ethnicity had, on the whole, an opposite effect. There has been a growth of identity politics within feminism, producing multiple positions representing the outlook of a particular group of women: Black feminism, Latina feminism, indigenous feminism, lesbian feminism, third-world feminism, etc.

Given the diversity of sexualities, regions, classes and nationalities, the result was a great multiplication of positions, standpoints and identities. It became conventional among middle-class White feminists in the

1990s to speak of 'feminisms' instead of 'feminism', in order to recognize diversity and disclaim privilege. New literatures emerged, even in the rich countries, of research and testimony from cultural backgrounds beyond the establishment. Lourdes Torres (1991), for instance, notes the growth of Latina writing in the United States, especially a new genre of autobiography. In Australia Sally Morgan's *My Place* (1987), an autobiography which turned into a reconstruction of family history over three generations, became celebrated as an account of Aboriginal women's experience.

With a rising awareness of race issues and ethnic difference, critical questions were raised about previous gender analysis, especially about accounts of oppression. White feminists had mainly seen the family as a site of women's oppression. But in a context of racism, the family (especially the extended family) might be a crucial asset for Black women, and women in recent immigrant communities. In very poor indigenous communities, women might hold more power or economic resources than men, or might feel that solidarity with the men of their communities is vital to survival. In Australia, for instance, Aboriginal women have been very reluctant to align themselves with White feminists or to make open criticisms of Aboriginal men.

The growth of attention to diversity within Western feminism was matched internationally. The Women's Liberation movement – partly because of American dominance of global communications – had a world-wide impact, triggering a revival or re-direction of other women's movements. In Japan, for instance, a range of women's organizations existed in the post-war years, based on unions, political parties, and a mothers' movement, but had lost vitality and become deeply factionalized. The Women's Liberation groups launched in 1970 provided a new agenda (including sexuality), new methods (including consciousness-raising), new language and a new energy (Tanaka 1977). Inter-governmental organizations picked up the rising attention to women's issues. The United Nations declared International Women's Year in 1975, then established the Decade for Women.

Several theoretical developments flowed from this. First was a feminist critique of international development aid programmes, dominated by men and mainly aiding men. There was a parallel critique of the gender-blindness of development studies as a field of knowledge. A critique was embodied in the United Nations' World Plan of Action, adopted at the first Decade for Women conference. Aid organizations have been forced to take the issue of gender inequality on board, though they still have difficulties dealing with gender equity (Staudt 1997).

Second, the problem of understanding the gender order on a world scale emerged. Texts such as Maria Mies's *Patriarchy and Accumulation on a World Scale* (1986), arising from the international debates, developed an analysis of colonialism and world capitalism as inherently gendered systems. Feminist analyses of contemporary international relations appeared, such as Cynthia Enloe's *Bananas, Beaches and Bases* (1990), showing the gender dimension in relations between states and international trade. The interplay of gender relations, migration and modern nationalisms has emerged as an important theme, in work like Nira Yuval-Davis's *Gender and Nation* (1997).

Third, global difference within feminism was emphasized. The United Nations conferences became the venue for powerful critiques of the hegemony of 'Western feminists'. The autonomy of local movements, the diversity of perspectives, and the distinctiveness of local situations were asserted. Since the UN conferences were inter-governmental events, officially representing states not movements, anti-feminist men and women were involved and some of the argument against Western feminism came from them. But an emphasis on global inequalities and cultural difference also came from feminist women, growing out of the experience of organizations and movements in situations as diverse as India, Japan and Mexico. As Chandra Talpade Mohanty (1991) observed in a world survey of this issue, it not only became necessary to recognize difference between first-world and third-world feminism. It became debatable whether there was a distinct position that one could call 'third-world feminism'. This concept seemed to be a survival from the colonial mindset which fundamentally distinguished 'the native' from the colonizing power, and lumped all 'natives' together.

In the wake of these developments, there has been a growing interest in post-colonial feminisms. In a comprehensive account of these discussions, *Re-orienting Western Feminisms*, Chilla Bulbeck (1998) surveys 'women's diversity in a postcolonial world' and confronts the radical consequences for Western feminists. To respond adequately to diversity is not just a matter of tacking 'anti-racism' onto an existing agenda. The issue is deeper, concerning ways of knowing and methods of action. It is a matter of learning 'to see oneself as others see one', learning to respect other experiences as genuinely other, learning to pluralize the view of the world, and learning to work in coalition modes.

This pluralization of perspectives has important implications for gender theory. If there are multiple feminisms, there must be multiple views of gender. Anyone who insists on a single overarching theory of gender can be seen as attempting to claim dominance for the viewpoint from which it was produced, and thus claiming intellectual, if not material, privilege. To some postmodern thinkers, any attempt to state general goals, or mobilize large numbers of people around common principles, reeks of totalitarianism.

Yet the opponents of feminism feel no such scruples. Religious absolutism seems to be reviving nicely in the 'postmodern' era. The market agenda steams ahead with confident claims to universal validity. In the face of the conservative reaction of the 1980s and 1990s, both feminist and gay activists have worried that an emphasis on diversity means growing division, and that deconstructive approaches to gender have de-mobilizing rather than energizing effects.

There are no easy solutions to these problems. I think, however, that a necessary response to them is to take a pragmatic approach to gender theory. 'Pragmatic' does not mean 'cynical' or 'anti-intellectual'; it means looking carefully at the uses of theory and research, at the effects of knowledge, and at the practical processes through which knowledge is created and disseminated. This is consistent, I think, with the views that led the Canadian sociologist Dorothy Smith (1987, 1990) to articulate a 'sociology for women' and a 'feminist sociology of knowledge'. The demand to pluralize perspectives as a result of global diversity should produce a richer and more accurate knowledge of gender, at the same time as it poses problems in connecting (or just living with) different perspectives. We might value any approach to gender that continues to be productive, in the sense of generating new insights, new research and new ideas for action.

From this point of view, the social perspectives which have been explored in this book seem to stand up well. They offer ways of thinking about global issues, and they continue to generate new kinds of research and ideas for practice.

An example is the exploration of men's place in gender relations. The exhaustion of sex role theory left the discussion of 'men's liberation' stranded. New beginnings were made in the mid-1980s, linking gay theory and feminist gender analysis. In the 1990s research on the social construction of masculinities multiplied in the rich countries, and policy discussions of issues ranging from men's health to boys' education and men's violence appeared. By the new decade these issues were being explored world-wide, as I have shown in *The Men and the Boys* (Connell 2000), and social research on masculinity was connecting to feminist discussions of gender as a global structure.

No account of very recent history can be more than provisional, so the last few pages are offered with caution. They cannot have covered all the developments that later, looking back from new perspectives, will register as important about this period of history. What I do claim with some confidence is that the issues outlined here are among those that do matter. Whatever new issues emerge, the problems of institutionalization, reaction, deconstruction, diversity and globalization are issues that must be incorporated into our understanding of gender.

8

Gender Politics

Personal politics

Four years ago Pam Benton, whose partner I had been for twenty-nine years, died of breast cancer. Breast cancer is almost entirely a women's disease. The medical specialists who treat it, however, are mostly men – as medical specialists mostly are in Australia. And they, naturally enough, have many of the attitudes and styles of interaction that men in the professions are likely to have.

Early in the treatment, Pam was referred to a prominent oncologist. Oncology is specialization in cancer, especially in its treatment through chemotherapy, the use of toxic drugs. This gentleman delivered himself of the opinion that if women would use their breasts for what they were intended for, they would not have so much trouble. Pam was furious, and did not consult him again.

There is, as the oncologist well knew, research evidence that rates of breast cancer are lower in women who have had babies early in life and have breast-fed. That is, so to speak, impersonal fact. (Though even with impersonal fact one may ask why researchers should have been concerned with that particular question rather than studying, say, cancer-causing chemicals in the environment.) The research finding was made into a gender insult – which the oncologist probably did not even realize was offensive – by his bland presumption that what women are 'for' is bearing babies. To him, if they had a different pattern of life, they were asking for what they got.

I tell this story not to attack doctors – I could tell of another senior medical man involved in Pam's treatment who was a model of thoughtfulness and care – but to emphasize how intimate and unavoidable gender politics is.

When the Women's Liberation movement said 'the personal is political', they were making this point. There is a gender politics in our most intimate relationships and decisions. Some issues about power and inequality are mundane, such as who does the dishes, who puts out the garbage and who writes the shopping list. Some are life-and-death, such as how childbirth and cancer treatment are done. Pam had been an activist in the women's movement over twenty years. We had been through the politics of dishwashing, among other things. She could see the gender politics in cancer medicine, and was not willing to be put down again.

The first tumour, which Pam discovered through routine screening, was so advanced that it required a mastectomy, surgical removal of the whole breast. This is a frightening (though not in itself life-threatening) operation which leaves a long scar where the breast had been. Recovering from the operation, Pam made contact with the support services available to mastectomy patients. It turned out that the main services provided were: provision of an artificial breast, individually tailored to replace the one that was lost; women coming to give grooming and dress advice so that the patient could present a normal, attractive feminine appearance to the world; and advice on how to restore family normality, overcome a husband's (expected) sexual disgust at a mutilated body, and deal with children's anxiety about their mother's being taken away from them.

This, too, is political. It is about placing women back in the culture of heterosexual femininity. It is about denying that normality has been rent, about women being held responsible for other people's emotional needs. And – not least – it is about restoring normal services to men.

But this politics operates at so deep a level of emotion that it is hardly perceptible as politics unless one is already aware of gender issues. Many women dedicate their lives to making a family and seeing it through the life-cycle. A sense of being desirable, of having an attractive or at least presentable body, is an important part of our culture's construction of womanhood. Women who are shocked by a major operation, and terrified by discovering they have a deadly disease, are unlikely to revolt against sexist stereotyping (though that is precisely what this 'service' involves), especially when it is presented to them as a form of care by other women.

Gender politics almost always has this dimension of intimacy, as well as involving larger social relations. That is one reason gender change can be so threatening, to many women as well as to many men. Impending changes can upset not only impersonal cultural or institutional arrangements. They also, at the same time and inseparably, upset people's cherished images of themselves, assumptions about personal relationships, and habits of everyday conduct.

Each year there is a women's march through central Sydney for International Women's Day. On one occasion, about fifteen years ago, Pam came home from the march quite shaken. I was in the kitchen when she came in, and she told me the story. A man, evidently hostile to the demonstration, had driven his car into the parade. The women managed to get out of the way, no one was injured – though that was luck. Someone could have been injured or even killed.

We talked about it over coffee. I cannot remember exactly how the conversation developed, though we must have soon found ourselves in conflict about the meaning of the event. What I remember all too clearly is that our disagreement kept escalating, until it blew up into one of the most troubling arguments we ever had.

To Pam this was not an isolated incident. It was part of a massive pattern of threat from men under which women live. She said 'They're trying to run us off the streets', and that was of course literally true in this case. Being a man, I had never been targeted this way. I hadn't been there, and Pam rightly argued that I had no business denying her interpretation of what she had seen. Women's lives had been threatened, and I seemed to her to be excusing the man who had done it.

For my part, I felt unjustly attacked, or attacked out of proportion to the issue. I wasn't denying that aggression had occurred. But I very much wanted *not* to reinforce Pam's sense of foreboding and fear, her sense of being always under threat of terrorism from men. Therefore I found myself trying to minimize the significance of what she had seen. I'm sure I also felt shaken, given a long commitment to feminist principles, to be lumped together in this argument with a sexist aggressor, or with all men as agents of patriarchy. Both of us went away shocked by the other's incomprehension and anger.

Pam was of course right in her main point. Women in Western urban society do live constantly under threat from men – threats that range from sexual harassment in the office and offensive remarks in the street, all the way to rape, domestic violence, and war. Being threatened is not an isolated or deviant experience. Very large numbers of women really have been jeered at, intimidated, bashed, raped, or pressured into sex.

But it wasn't just the knowledge of these broad facts that made our argument so emotional and difficult. It was Pam's experience of this specific piece of intimidation, my not sharing the experience, and my failure – because I have had few experiences of being intimidated – to grasp its meaning imaginatively. She had come home frightened and disturbed, and I had not given her the support she wanted.

But the personal level of politics is not only a source of difficulty and division. It can also be a basis of solidarity and a source of energy and strength. The International Women's Day march from which Pam had returned is a case in point. These marches are generally occasions of joy and exhilaration. The personal connections made among the women present aren't just an incidental bonus. They are part of the solidarity of women, the process of creating strength, that is the point of the march.

Pam wrote a short story about an IWD march (Benton 1984). This gives the thoughts of a faint-hearted feminist on the bus going to the demonstration, hearing that the bus is being diverted on account of a 'procession of ladies':

> What *I* want are some good songs. Usually I just have a long talk to someone I haven't seen for ages.
>
> Some years there have been good slogans though. Adelaide, 1976: 'Purge the internal patriarch'. All the way down Rundle Mall, along North Terrace past the Adelaide Club, back to Victoria Square.
>
> Silence behind me.
> In front, and on both sides, the grumbles:
> 'Why can't they wait til the shops shut and not interfere with other people?'
> 'What did he say it was about?' 'Oh some march. That anti-union mob.'. . .
> SHIT. HAVE TO DO SOMETHING.
> I rehearse: standing, walking to the front, turning, facing the hostility: 'It's not a *ladies'* procession. It's International Women's Day. You should be with us. We're marching to celebrate . . .'
> Christ, what *is* it?
> Suppose the media are doing 'why are you here?' interviews? Garment workers, first women's strike, equal pay, match girls . . . ?
>
> I get off one block earlier than necessary.
> I'm no good at public speeches.
>
> Anyway, they were handing out song sheets to the marchers.

The politics of Gay Liberation similarly combined the personal and the structural. Collective actions in the public domain produced similar feelings of exhilaration and common purpose. Gay politics, however, involved another dimension as well, the process of 'coming out'. Acknowledging gayness to oneself, one's family, one's friends and work-mates, can be a difficult and protracted business. Large adjustments and realignments have to be made. The collective process of establishing a gay community, a gay identity in the culture, and a gay presence in politics and economic life, both depends on the individual process and supports it.

A decade after the emergence of Gay Liberation, at a time when the effervescent radicalism of the first years had been tamed, or absorbed into the business of building gay communities, gay politics was trans-formed by the HIV/AIDS epidemic. In the struggle to deal with AIDS, the link between the personal and the structural was reconfigured around new issues in body politics. The response has been vividly described by Dennis Altman in *Power and Community: Organizational and Cultural Responses to AIDS* (1994).

On the one hand a whole new set of relationships, between gay com-munities and individuals and health authorities and doctors, had to be negotiated. On the other hand, a hostile symbolic politics about infect-ion, pollution and uncleanness, whipped up by the homophobic reli-gious right and tabloid media, had to be dealt with. Both jobs had to be done in a context of illness, bereavement and fear. The fact that gay com-munities have survived this terrible crisis is an impressive testimony to the culture and solidarity created in the collective coming out of the 1970s.

Gender politics may occur, and generate some of this energy, without a gender- or sexuality-based movement. Nancy Naples, in *Community Activism and Feminist Politics* (1998), has recently collected American examples of women's activism, especially in working-class communities. The range of issues is impressive: schools, toxic waste, poverty, domes-tic violence, racism, housing, support of strike action, ethnic community needs. The bases of this activism often lie in women's position in the gender division of labour, for instance issues that arise in childcare, or feeding a family, or sustaining health. The gendered networks that develop through women's work can provide the framework of political mobilization.

Some of the same energy can also be found in anti-feminist politics. The gun lobby provides an example. The cultural masculinization of weapons is a fact of culture, not nature, which must be constantly regenerated. A fascinating and frightening study by William Gibson, *Warrior Dreams* (1994), shows some of the mechanisms. Gibson traces the cult of weapons in the hypermasculine 'paramilitary culture' in the United States, which grew after the US defeat in Vietnam. Local bases such as gun clubs and recreational hunting have been worked up, by entrepreneurs and activists, into training camps, militias and sometimes armed sects, as well as the broader 'gun lobby' represented by the National Rifle Association.

These groups exist in a larger context: the arms manufacturing industry (which funds some of their activities), the military, and the intersection of the two that President Eisenhower called 'the military-industrial complex'. Arms dealing ranges from government-to-government sales of extremely expensive airborne weapons systems to the private circulation of handguns, shotguns and hunting rifles in countries whose governments permit arms sales, or cannot prevent them. The largest part of the arms trade is the legal equipping of military and paramilitary forces.

The weapons come wrapped in social forms, and the organizations involved have gender regimes. Military forces are patriarchal institutions. Fascinating research has been done by Frank Barrett (1996) on gender patterns in US naval officer training. He documents an oppressive but efficient regime – emphasizing competition, physical hardness, conformity, and a sense of elite membership – designed to produce a narrowly defined hegemonic masculinity, and therefore creating serious problems for women trainees. The statements by officers who have gone through it show that such a training regime penetrates to basic feelings about the self. The training works by linking the sense of personal worth to the needs of an organization that specializes in violence. Similar patterns have been found in research on military masculinities in Germany (Seifert 1993) and other countries. It is clear that this construction of masculinity is a widespread feature of military life.

By disseminating this organizational culture, the arms trade is a vector of the globalization of gender, much as the international state is (see chapter 6). Indeed, the two overlap, since the arms trade is connected to the globally linked military and intelligence apparatuses of the major powers. In a world perspective, the modest gains of women's representation in bureaucracies and parliaments at a national level may well be outweighed by the growth of the machinery of masculine violence at an international level.

The patriarchal dividend and gender harm

What is political about gender? In one of the foundation texts of Women's Liberation, *Sexual Politics* (1972: 23), Kate Millett defined 'politics' as 'power-structured relationships, arrangements whereby one group of persons is controlled by another'. What made her argument scandalous was that she applied this definition to the relation between women and men.

The relation of power is only one of the inequalities described by Millett, and by the hundreds of researchers who have filled in the details since she wrote. Systematic inequalities exist in a range of resources, from income and wealth to social honour and cultural authority (see chapter 4). Inequalities define interests. Those benefiting from inequalities have an interest in defending them. Those who bear the costs have an interest in ending them.

Gender inequalities are usually expressed in terms of women's lack of resources relative to men's. For instance, in chapter 1 above I cited statistics that show women's average incomes, world-wide, as 56 per cent of men's. While this way of presenting information makes sense in establishing a case for reform, it continues the bad old habit of defining women by their relation to men. We should also turn the equation around and consider the surplus of resources made available to men. The same figures, read this way, show men's average incomes, world-wide, as 179 per cent of women's.

I call this surplus the *patriarchal dividend*: the advantage to men as a group from maintaining an unequal gender order. The patriarchal dividend is reduced as overall gender equality grows. Monetary benefits are not the only kind of benefit. Others are authority, respect, service, safety, housing, access to institutional power, and control over one's own life.

It is important to note that the patriarchal dividend is the benefit to men *as a group*. Individual men may get more of it than others, or less, or none, depending on their location in the social order. A wealthy businessman draws large dividends from the gendered accumulation process in advanced capitalism; an unemployed working-class man may draw no economic benefits at all. Specific groups of men may be excluded collectively from parts of the patriarchal dividend. Thus gay men, broadly speaking, are excluded from the authority and respect attached to men who embody hegemonic forms of masculinity.

Some women also participate in the patriarchal dividend, generally by being married to wealthy men. Such women get dividends from the gendered accumulation process (e.g. live on a profit stream generated by women's underpaid and unpaid labour), and are able to benefit directly from other women doing the domestic labour in their households. This became a political scandal in the United States in 1993, when the Clinton administration attempted to appoint several bourgeois women to senior positions, only to find they had failed to pay taxes on their immigrant women houseworkers.

The patriarchal dividend is the main stake in contemporary gender politics. Its scale makes patriarchy worth defending. Those sex-role reformers in the 1970s who attempted to persuade men that Women's Liberation was good for them, and therefore tried to start a parallel Men's Liberation movement, were undoubtedly right about the costs of hegemonic masculinity. Men would be safer not fighting, would be healthier without competitive stress, would live longer without the cigarettes and booze, and would be better off in mutually respectful relations with women. But the same reformers hopelessly underestimated the patriarchal dividend, missing what men stood to gain from current arrangements in terms of power, economic advantage, prestige, etc. Thus they missed the interest most men have in sustaining – and, where necessary, defending – the current gender order.

To argue that the current gender order should be changed is to claim that it does more harm than good. The harm of gender is first and foremost in the system of inequality that produces a patriarchal dividend, a system in which women and girls are exploited, discredited, and made vulnerable to abuse and attack. Those feminists who think that gender is inherently about inequality, who in effect see the patriarchal dividend as the core of gender relations, logically seek to abolish gender. Social justice would require no less.

The harm of gender is also found in specific patterns of practice formed in the gender order that are given power to affect the world by the collective resources of the society. Contemporary hegemonic masculinity, to take the most striking case, is dangerous regardless of the patriarchal dividend. It is dangerous because it is directly connected with inter-personal violence, and because in alliance with state and corporate power it drives arms races, strip mining and deforestation, hostile labour relations, and the abuse of technologies from motor transport to genetic engineering.

But if gender in these respects is harmful, it is in other respects a source of pleasure, creativity and other things we greatly value. Gender organizes our sexual relationships, which are sources of delight and growth. Gender is integral to our cultural riches, from *Noh* plays to rap and reggae. The joys and strains of gender relations are among the most potent sources of cultural creation.

I would argue, then, that the stakes in gender politics include the value of gender as well as its harm. Gender politics has the possibility of shaping pleasures as well as distributing resources, and making possible a more creative culture.

Given these possibilities, 'gender politics' has to be understood as more than an interest-group struggle over inequalities. In the most general sense, gender politics is about the *steering* of the gender order in history. It represents the struggle to have the endless re-creation of gender relations through practice turn out a particular way.

It is easy to recognize that a struggle over economic resources is 'political', less easy to think that the reconstruction of personality is. But if I am right that personality is a configuration of practice in the same sense – though at a different level – as the gender regime of an institution (see chapter 4), then struggles to change personality are equally political. Existential psychoanalysis and cultural radicalism in the 1960s produced the insight that there is a 'politics of experience' (to quote the title of a famous book by R. D. Laing, 1968), an idea that connects directly to the feminist argument that 'the personal is political'.

The masculinity therapy of the mythopoetic men's movement, then, is political not just because of its patriarchal imagery, but because of what it centrally is, an attempt to create or restore a particular gender configuration of practice. Feminist 'consciousness-raising' (out of which masculinity therapy arose) does not just lead to politics, it *is* politics. Confrontational discipline in families and schools, and confrontational policing ('zero tolerance', three-strikes laws, more prisons and harsher prison regimes), are equally political, applications of power intended to shape personality. These are practices which call out 'protest masculinity' among many working-class and ethnic minority boys and young men.

Gender politics, whether at the institutional or the personal level, always represent a collective project. This is easy enough to see in the case of modern feminism and gay politics. Both are social movements directed against an oppressive established order. But social movements are not the only form gender politics can take.

What feminism is fighting against, for the most part, is not a countervailing social movement. Though there have been efforts to create Men's Rights groups or 'masculinist' movements, most such attempts have been small-scale, cranky and short-lived. The more successful 'men's movements' in recent years have pursued agendas of therapy (the 'mythopoetic movement'), racial justice or religion (the 'Million Man March', the 'Promise Keepers'), and gender reform aligned with feminism (men's anti-violence groups). These agendas are either marginal to, or opposed to, the defence of patriarchy.

This is not to say the defence of patriarchy has been neglected. But the collective agency of dominant groups of men is expressed in other ways than social movements. Patriarchal power normally operates through the routine functioning of the institutions in which the dominance of men is embedded – corporations, churches, mass media, legal systems and governments. To the extent the dominant interest needs articulation, it is done by establishment figures (popes, generals, chief justices, chairmen of the board) who declare the perspective of authority, or by non-establishment media figures (Rush Limbaugh, John Laws) whose job it is to ridicule the opposition (for instance, by attacks on 'political correctness').

Thus the defence of hegemonic masculinity normally goes on as a collective project without a social movement. In situations of dire upheaval, however, a social movement with exceptionally clear-cut masculinity politics may emerge. The most striking case is fascism. The Italian and German fascist movements of the 1920s and 1930s are better known for their class, nationalist and racist projects. But these movements, whose activists had often been soldiers, also attempted the restoration of a hegemonic masculinity severely disrupted by war and economic upheaval. The neo-nazi and racist fringe groups of the 1980s and 1990s have tried to re-create aggressive gender politics along with the rest of the package.

Gender politics, then, take a variety of forms. It is not helpful to regard *every* aspect of gender as 'political'. That would foreclose what ought to be an empirical question – what in any given situation is actually involved in the 'steering' of the gender order. But there is no doubt that gender politics are generally complex and extensive, and laden with consequences for humanity. In the final section of this chapter I will explore some of these consequences as they appear on the world scale.

Gender politics on a world scale

A structure of social relations, having come into existence in history, is open to change in history. A structure of inequality can, in principle, move in a democratic direction. Whether it does so or not is a question of social struggle. The analysis of the global gender order in chapter

6 suggests two basic arenas of struggle for democratization: in global institutions, and in the interactions between local gender orders.

Democratization in the first arena, global institutions, is straightforward in concept if difficult in practice. It is the same kind of process as the democratization of organizations at the national or local level. In practical terms it means:

- attempting to get equal employment opportunity in transnational corporations,
- ending the misogyny and homophobia in international media,
- gaining equal representation of women and men in international forums and agencies,
- ending gender discrimination in international labour markets,
- creating anti-discrimination norms in the public culture, etc.

A world-wide agency of change is already in existence. There is a women's movement presence in international meetings (recently described by Deborah Stienstra, 2000). This works to some extent through official delegations, more consistently through the growing presence of non-government organizations, now a recognized category of participants in United Nations activities. Women's units or programmes have been set up in some international organizations, such as UNESCO, and are now coordinated through the United Nations Division for the Advancement of Women. There is also a certain international presence of gay and lesbian movements, and (on a smaller scale) pro-feminist men's groups.

These social forces have been able to place some issues about gender relations on the agendas of diplomacy and the international state. In doing so they have been greatly assisted by the 'human rights' agenda in international organizations. The United Nations set up a Commission on the Status of Women as early as 1946. Article 2 of the 1948 Universal Declaration of Human Rights banned discrimination on the basis of sex, as well as race, religion, etc. It has been followed by specific agreements about the rights of women, culminating in the Convention on the Elimination of All Forms of Discrimination against Women, introduced in 1979. The human rights agenda has been far more important than the 'men's movement' in winning support for gender equality from men in international organizations – support that has been vital in creating the spaces in which women's groups have operated.

Among the consequences of this pressure are: increased recognition of the gender dimension in development aid, and concern by aid agencies to support the interests of women; the growing global commitment to the secondary and higher education of women; a growing concern with gendered violence and with gender issues in peacekeeping; recognition of the voices of women and gay men in the global programme against AIDS.

Nevertheless the forces pushing for gender democratization are still weak in relation to the scale of the problem. The most important limit is that they still have very little influence in transnational corporations and global markets. A notional obedience to anti-discrimination laws in the countries where they have their head offices does not prevent transnational corporations maintaining sharp gender divisions in their workforce in reality. Their characteristic search for cheap labour around the world often leads them, and their local suppliers, to exploit the weak industrial position of women workers. This is especially the case where unions are hampered or where governments have set up 'free trade zones' to attract international capital, or where there is a demand for cheap domestic labour (Fuentes and Ehrenreich 1983, Marchand and Runyan 2000).

Even in public sector agencies there is far from being a unified force for change. Conferences of the UN Decade for Women, for instance, have been vital in articulating world agendas for gender reform. But among the national delegations attending them have been some headed or controlled by men, some headed by women with no commitment to gender equality, and some dominated by patriarchal ideologies actively opposed to gender equality. These conferences have been the occasion of sharp conflict over issues such as abortion and lesbianism. Even the concept of 'gender' was under attack at the 1995 Beijing conference, because it was supposed by right-wing forces to be a code word for feminism (Benden and Goetz 1998).

Some of these divisions arise from the second dimension of global gender politics, the relations between local gender orders. As observed in chapter 7, during the 1980s it became common to speak of 'feminisms' instead of 'feminism', and divergences between first-world and third-world feminisms were widely canvassed. While support for equality between women and men could be seen as a mark of modernity, it could also be seen as a sign of cultural imperialism. Certain forms of Western feminism which emphasized gender difference and women's autonomy aroused opposition from women who did not want to be separated from the men of their communities in struggles against racism, colonial or neo-colonial domination (Bulbeck 1988).

Even conceptualizing a democratic agenda in this dimension is difficult. The interplay between gender orders arises historically from a system of global domination, that is, imperialism and colonialism. A democratic agenda must oppose the inequalities that have been inherited from this system, between global 'North' and global 'South'. This is a strong point made by those women who argue against separate political organization.

Yet the gender alignments here are complex. The colonial system, and the globalized world economy, have been run by men. But the anti-colonial struggle, too, was almost everywhere led by men. Post-colonial regimes have generally been patriarchal, and have sometimes been violently misogynist or homophobic. For instance, Robert Mugabe, leader of a bitter struggle to end colonialism in Rhodesia, as president of Zimbabwe is running the most openly homophobic campaign of any government in the contemporary world.

In post-colonial regimes the men of local elites have often been complicit with businessmen from the metropole in the exploitation of women's labour. Multinational corporations could not operate as they do without this co-operation. In places like the Philippines and Thailand men of local elites have been central in the creation of international sex trade destinations. Arms trafficking similarly involves an interplay between the men who control local military forces and governments, and the men who run arms manufacturing corporations in the metropole.

A further complexity, explored in Dennis Altman's important new book *Global Sex* (2001), is that the interplay between gender orders within global capitalism has produced a range of novel identities and patterns of relationship, sexual communities and political processes. They belong neither to local nor metropolitan cultures, but in a sense to both – and more exactly, to the new global society that is emerging.

The criterion of democratic action, in this dimension of the world gender order, must be what democracy always means: moving towards equality of participation, power and respect. The difficulty is that this criterion must apply at the same time to relations in the local gender order and to relations between gender orders. The resulting complexities are so great that gender-democratic practice must often be ambiguous or contradictory.

For instance, action to strengthen the bargaining power of women factory and agricultural workers may weaken the position of the local bourgeoisie in the global economy. A weakened national economy may (as the countries of Eastern Europe and the former Soviet Union have found) push many women towards prostitution. Attempts to strengthen the position of homosexual men and women by public campaigns and actions to reinforce a sense of community may also expose them to attack from political leaders who picture homosexuality as Western decadence.

Yet progressive movements cannot evacuate these arenas simply because democratic practice is difficult. Anti-democratic forces are certainly not evacuating them. In many parts of the world the rise of feminism has been followed by a backlash, as the journalist Susan Faludi (1991) argued in the case of the United States. This has mostly taken the shape of informal cultural movements which reinforce the supremacy of men, argue that gender hierarchy is biologically fixed, or claim that women's advancement is damaging to the family, to children, or to religion. In the 1990s a campaign against 'political correctness', begun in the United States and circulated internationally by neo-conservative networks, attacked measures against sexism on the grounds that these violate free speech, and programmes for women on the grounds that these discriminate against men.

Political agendas reflecting these arguments have been advanced in individual countries, from the de-funding of women's groups in Australia to the restriction of abortion rights in the United States. They have also been pursued in international forums, such as the Cairo international conference on Population and Development in 1994. At this conference an alliance against women's reproductive freedom was put together by the Vatican, certain Catholic countries influenced by the Vatican, and some Islamic governments including Iran (though in this case the alliance had little effect). Backlash ideas are also given wide publicity in international media.

Perhaps more powerful than all backlash movements put together is the impact of neo-liberalism. This has been the dominant movement in world politics in the last two decades. Neo-liberalism was already on the rise before the collapse of Stalinist regimes in the Soviet Union and its satellites around 1989, but was given a tremendous boost by those events. Neo-liberal agendas, closely associated with the power of global markets, have attempted to 'roll back' the state through deregulation of markets, privatization of public services, and reduction of public expenditure. In international finance, agencies such as the International Monetary Fund have used a continuing debt crisis to force neo-liberal policies on many governments which were needing loans, or needing to re-finance old loans.

The resultant weakening of welfare states has broadly been to the detriment of women. Because of the gender division of labour and inequalities of income, women have been more dependent than men on public services and on income transfers through the state. Men control almost all market-based institutions, such as corporations, and acquire most of the income distributed through markets, such as salaries and wages. Neo-liberalism, in exalting the power of markets, has thus tended to restore the power and privilege of men. It is not surprising that the installation of a market economy in former communist countries has been followed by worsening conditions for women.

The 1990s saw the appearance, particularly in the rich countries, of 'men's movements' of several kinds. These movements have mostly been inspired by what I have called the 'toxicity' of the gender order. They have offered psychological or religious solutions to the damage (the 'wounds', as some put it) suffered by men. Most have had little to say about gender democracy. The main exceptions are the small but active men's anti-violence movement, and the longest-established 'men's movement', the gay community politics descended from Gay Liberation. Gay men's groups have struggled against prejudice and homophobic violence, and have in some situations (though not all) been aligned with feminism.

At present there is a spectrum of masculinity politics in the rich countries ranging from explicitly pro-feminist to distinctly anti-feminist; the American sociologist Michael Messner has provided a useful map of this terrain in *The Politics of Masculinities* (1997). Surveys of broader populations of men have found similar divisions. For instance, a 1988 survey of men in Norway found them dividing into three groups of roughly equal size, one-third supporting gender equality, one-third negative towards women and equality issues, and one-third in the middle (Holter 1997: 131–5). A German survey in 1998 also found a national sample of men dividing into 'new' vs. 'traditional', plus two intermediate groups, 'pragmatic' and 'uncertain' (Zulehner and Volz 1998). I do not know of any study which has looked at the gender ideologies of men in international organizations, but I think it probable there is a similar range of views.

The diversity of men's gender outlooks makes possible a range of political responses and alliances. However strong the combination of neo-liberalism and gender backlash is in particular cases, there are also possibilities for progressive politics among men, and possible alliances with women's groups. This can be seen, for instance, in international discussions of violence and peacemaking, where feminist concerns with gendered violence have recently been brought together with masculinity research and men's groups (Breines, Connell and Eide 2000).

We are still in the early stages of the struggle for gender democracy on a world scale. As that struggle develops, gender theory and research will have a number of roles to play.

Simply documenting the patterns of gender inequality, as Valdés and Gomáriz (1995: 12–13) argue, helps overcome the invisibility of women and the taken-for-granted character of gender oppression. Providing accounts of how gender inequality is produced can be important in contesting the ideologies that present gender inequality as biologically driven or god-given. Documenting changes in gender relations and struggles for gender democracy (e.g. Naples 1998) is a significant way of circulating knowledge and models of action, and thus disseminating tools for democratic politics. Gender theory, specifically, makes it possible to communicate ideas between people in different situations.

None of this means that familiar Western models of gender can or should be imposed on the rest of the world. As feminism itself has found, one cannot go global without being profoundly changed. Gender theory and research will need to reconsider themselves again and again, in the light of the diverse cultures and forms of knowledge that appear in world gender politics. Given willingness to learn, gender theory and research can play a significant role in making a more democratic world.

References

Adams, Annmarie, and Peta Tancred. 2000. *Designing Women: Gender and the Architectural Profession*, toronto: University of Toronto Press.

Adler, Alfred. 1992 [1927]. *Understanding Human Nature*, translated by C. Brett. Oxford: Oneworld.

Altman, Dennis. 1972. *Homosexual: Oppression and Liberation*. Sydney: Angus & Robertson.

——1982. *The Homosexualization of America, the Americanization of the Homosexual*. New York: St Martin's Press.

——1994. *Power and Community: Organizational and Cultural Responses to AIDS*. London: Taylor & Francis.

——1996. 'Rupture or continuity? the internationalization of gay identities', *Social Text* 48: 77–94.

——2001. *Global Sex*. Chicago: University of Chicago Press.

American Association of University Women. 1992. *How Schools Shortchange Girls: A Study of Major Findings on Girls and Education*. USA: American Association of University Women Educational Foundation.

Arnot, Madeleine, Miriam David, and Gaby Weiner. 1999. *Closing the Gender Gap: Postwar Education and Social Change*. Cambridge: Polity.

Banner, Lois W. 1983. *American Beauty*. Chicago: University of Chicago Press.

Barker, Pat. 1992. *Regeneration*. London: Penguin.

Barrett, Frank J. 1996. 'Gender strategies of women naval officers', in *Women's Research and Education Institute: Conference on Women in Uniformed Services*. Washington, DC.

Beauvoir, Simone de. 1972 [1949]. *The Second Sex*. Harmondsworth: Penguin.

Bebel, August. 1971 [1879]. *Women under Socialism [Die Frau und der Sozialismus]*. New York: Schocken Books.

Bem, Sandra L. 1974. 'The measurement of psychological androgyny', *Journal of Consulting and Clinical Psychology* 42: 155–62.

Benden, Sally, and Anne-Marie Goetz. 1998. 'Who needs [sex] when you can have [gender]? conflicting discourses on gender at Beijing', in *Feminist Visions of Development: Gender, Analysis and Policy*, edited by C. Jackson and R. Pearson. London: Routledge.

Benton, Pam [writing as Dale Walker]. 1984. 'Procession of ladies', pp. 100–3 in *And So Say All of Us: Stories by Australian Women*, edited by P. McNeill and M. McShea. Adelaide: Second Back Row Press.

Bettencourt, B. Ann, and Norman Miller. 1996. 'Gender differences in aggression as a function of provocation: a meta-analysis', *Psychological Bulletin* 119: 422–7.

Bottomley, Gillian. 1992. *From Another Place: Migration and the Politics of Culture*. Melbourne: Cambridge University Press.

Breines, Ingeborg, Robert Connell, and Ingrid Eide, eds. 2000. *Male Roles, Masculinities and Violence: A Culture of Peace Perspective*. Paris: UNESCO Publishing.

Bulbeck, Chilla. 1988. *One World Women's Movement*. London: Pluto Press.

——1998. *Re-orienting Western Feminisms: Women's Diversity in a Postcolonial World*. Cambridge: Cambridge University Press.

Burton, Clare. 1987. 'Merit and gender: organisations and the mobilisation of masculine bias', *Australian Journal of Social Issues* 22: 424–35.

Butler, Judith. 1990. *Gender Trouble: Feminism and the Subversion of Identity*. New York: Routledge.

Caplan, Pat, ed. 1987. *The Cultural Construction of Sexuality*. London: Tavistock.

Carrigan, Tim, Robert Connell, and John Lee. 1985. 'Toward a new sociology of masculinity', *Theory and Society* 14: 551–604.

Chapkis, Wendy. 1997. *Live Sex Acts: Women Performing Erotic Labor*. New York: Routledge.

Chodorow, Nancy. 1978. *The Reproduction of Mothering: Psychoanalysis and the Sociology of Gender*. Berkeley: University of California Press.

——1994. *Femininities, Masculinities, Sexualities: Freud and Beyond*. Lexington, Ky.: University Press of Kentucky.

Clark, Jeffrey. 1997. 'State of desire: transformations in Huli sexuality', pp. 191–211 in *Sites of Desire: Sexualities in Asia and the Pacific*, edited by L. Manderson and M. Jolly. Chicago: University of Chicago Press.

Cockburn, Cynthia. 1983. *Brothers: Male Dominance and Technological Change*. London: Pluto Press.

Collinson, David, David Knights, and Margaret Collinson. 1990. *Managing to Discriminate*. London: Routledge.

Comte, Auguste. 1875–7 [1851–4]. *System of Positive Polity, or Treatise on Sociology.* London: Longmans Green.

Connell, R. W. 1983. *Which Way is Up? Essays on Sex, Class and Culture* Sydney: Allen & Unwin.

——1987. *Gender and Power: Society, the Person and Sexual Politics.* Cambridge: Polity.

——1995. *Masculinities.* Cambridge: Polity.

——2000. *The Men and the Boys.* Cambridge: Polity.

Connell, R. W., T. Schofield, L. Walker, J. Wood, D. Butland, J. Fisher and J. Bowyer. 1999. *Men's Health: A Research Agenda and Background Report.* Canberra: Commonwealth Department of Health and Aged Care.

Cooper, Harris, and Larry V. Hedges, eds. 1994. *The Handbook of Research Synthesis.* New York: Russell Sage Foundation.

Corman, June, Meg Luxton, David Livingstone and Wally Secombe. 1993. *Recasting Steel Labour: the Stelco Story.* Halifax: Fernwood Publishing.

Crawford, Mary. 1995. *Talking Difference: On Gender and Language.* London: Sage.

Crook, John, and Andrew Harding. 1997. *Gun Massacres in Australia: The Case for Gun Control.* Melbourne: Gun Control Australia Inc.

Cummings, Katherine. 1992. *Katherine's Diary: The Story of a Transsexual.* Melbourne: Heinemann.

Daly, Mary. 1978. *Gyn/Ecology: The Metaethics of Radical Feminism.* Boston: Beacon Press.

Darwin, Charles. 1928 [1859]. *The Origin of Species.* London: Dent.

Davidoff, Leonore, and Catherine Hall. 1987. *Family Fortunes: Men & Women of the English Middle Class 1780–1850.* London: Hutchinson.

Davies, Bronwyn. 1993. *Shards of Glass: Children Reading and Writing beyond Gendered Identities.* Sydney: Allen & Unwin.

De Cecco, John. 1990. 'Sex and more sex: a critique of the Kinsey conception of human sexuality', pp. 367–86 in *Homosexuality/Heterosexuality: Concepts of Sexual Orientation*, edited by D. McWhirter et al. New York: Oxford University Press.

Degler, Carl N. 1990. 'Darwinians confront gender; or, there is more to it than history', pp. 33–45 in *Theoretical Perspectives on Sexual Difference*, edited by D. L. Rhode. New Haven: Yale University Press.

Delphy, Christine. 1984. *Close to Home: A Materialist Analysis of Women's Oppression.* London: Hutchinson.

Dobash, R. Emerson, and Russell P. Dobash. 1992. *Women, Violence and Social Change.* London: Routledge.

Donaldson, Mike. 1991. *Time of our Lives: Labour and Love in the Working Class.* Sydney: Allen & Unwin.

Dowsett, Gary W. 1996. *Practicing Desire: Homosexual Sex in the Era of AIDS.* Stanford, Calif.: Stanford University Press.

Draper, Joan. 1993. 'We're back with Gobbo: the re-establishment of gender relations following a school merger', pp. 49–74 in *Gender and Ethnicity in Schools: Ethnographic Accounts*, edited by P. Woods and M. Hammersley. London: Routledge/Open University.

Dull, Diana and Candace West. 1991. 'Accounting for cosmetic surgery: the accomplishment of gender', *Social Problems* 38: 54–70.

Dunne, Gillian A. 1997. *Lesbian Lifestyles: Women's Work and the Politics of Sexuality*. Basingstoke: Macmillan.

Eagly, Alice H. 1987. *Sex Differences in Social Behavior: A Social-Role Interpretation*. Hillside, NJ: Lawrence Erlbaum.

Easthope, Antony. 1986. *What a Man's Gotta Do: The Masculine Myth in Popular Culture*. London: Paladin.

Eisenstein, Hester. 1996. *Inside Agitators: Australian Femocrats and the State*. Sydney: Allen & Unwin.

Engels, Friedrich. 1970 [1884]. *The Origin of The Family, Private Property and the State*, pp. 191–334 in *Marx/Engels Selected Works*. Moscow: Progress Publishers.

Enloe, Cynthia. 1990. *Bananas, Beaches and Bases: Making Feminist Sense of International Politics*. Berkeley: University of California Press.

Epstein, Cynthia Fuchs. 1988. *Deceptive Distinctions: Sex, Gender and the Social Order*. New Haven: Yale University Press.

Erikson, Erik H. 1950. *Childhood and Society*. London: Imago.

Essen, Mineke van. 2000. 'Gender in beweging: over pedagogiek en sekse in de Lichamelijke Opvoeding van de Twinstigste EEUW', *Tijdschrift voor Genderstudies* 3: 25–35.

Fairweather, Hugh. 1976. 'Sex differences in cognition', *Cognition* 4: 231–80.

Faludi, Susan. 1991. *Backlash: The Undeclared War against American Women*. New York: Crown.

Fausto-Sterling, Anne. 2000. *Sexing the Body: Gender Politics and the Construction of Sexuality*. New York: Basic Books.

Firestone, Shulamith. 1971. *The Dialectic of Sex*. London: Paladin.

Foley, Douglas. 1990. *Learning Capitalist Culture: Deep in the Heart of Tejas*. Philadelphia: University of Pennsylvania Press.

Foucault, Michel. 1977. *Discipline and Punish: The Birth of the Prison*, translated by A. Sheridan. New York: Pantheon.

——1980. *The History of Sexuality, Volume I: An Introduction*. New York: Vintage.

Franzway, Suzanne. forthcoming. *Sexual Politics and Greedy Institutions*. Sydney: Pluto Press.

Franzway, Suzanne, Dianne Court, and R. W. Connell. 1989. *Staking a Claim: Feminism, Bureaucracy and the State*. Sydney: Allen & Unwin.

Fraser, Nancy. 1989. *Unruly Practices: Power, Discourse and Gender in Con-*

temporary Social Theory. Cambridge: Polity and Minneapolis: University of Minnesota Press.

Frazer, J. G. 1890. *The Golden Bough: A Study in Comparative Religion.* London: Macmillan.

Fregoso, Rosa Linda. 1993. *The Bronze Screen: Chicana and Chicano Film Culture.* Minneapolis: University of Minnesota Press.

Freud, Sigmund. 1953 [1900]. *The Interpretation of Dreams*, in *Complete Psychological Works*, vols 4–5. London: Hogarth.

——1953 [1905]. 'Fragment of an analysis of a case of hysteria', in *Complete Psychological Works*, vol. 7. London: Hogarth.

——1953 [1905]. *Three Essays on the Theory of Sexuality*, in *Complete Psychological Works*, vol. 7. London: Hogarth.

——1955 [1918]. 'From the history of an infantile neurosis', in *Complete Psychological Works*, vol. 17. London: Hogarth.

——1961 [1930]. *Civilization and its Discontents*, in *Complete Psychological Works*, vol. 21. London: Hogarth.

Fuentes, Annette, and Barbara Ehrenreich. 1983. *Women in the Global Factory.* Boston: South End Press.

Gagnon, John H., and William Simon. 1974. *Sexual Conduct: The Social Sources of Human Sexuality.* London: Hutchinson.

Geary, David C. 1998. *Male, Female: The Evolution of Human Sex Differences.* Washington, DC: American Psychological Association.

Gee, James Paul, Glynda Hull, and Colin Lankshear. 1996. *The New Work Order: Behind the Language of the New Capitalism.* Sydney: Allen & Unwin.

Gender Equality Ombudsman (Norway). 1997. 'The Father's Quota: Information Sheet on Parental Leave Entitlements.' Oslo.

Gero, Joan M., and Margaret W. Conkey, eds. 1991. *Engendering Archaeology: Women and Prehistory.* Oxford: Blackwell.

Ghoussoub, Mai, and Emma Sinclair-Webb, eds. 2000. *Imagined Masculinities: Male Identity and Culture in the Modern Middle East.* London: Saqi Books.

Gibson, James William. 1994. *Warrior Dreams: Paramilitary Culture in Post-Vietnam America.* New York: Hill and Wang.

Gierycz, Dorota. 1999. 'Women in decision-making: can we change the status quo?', in *Towards a Woman's Agenda for a Culture of Peace*, edited by I. Breines, D. Gierycz and B. A. Reardon. Paris: UNESCO.

Gilligan, Carol. 1982. *In a Different Voice: Psychological Theory and Women's Development.* Cambridge, Mass.: Harvard University Press.

Glass Ceiling Commission. 1995a. *Good for Business: Making Full Use of the Nation's Human Capital. The Environmental Scan.* Washington, DC: Federal Glass Ceiling Commission.

——1995b. *A Solid Investment: Making Full Use of the Nation's Human*

Capital. Recommendations. Washington, DC: Federal Glass Ceiling Commission.

Glucksmann, Miriam [writing as Ruth Cavendish]. 1982. *Women on the Line.* London: Routledge & Kegan Paul.

Glucksmann, Miriam. 1990. *Women Assemble: Women Workers and the New Industries in Inter-war Britain.* London: Routledge.

Goldberg, Steven. 1993. *Why Men Rule: A Theory of Male Dominance.* Chicago: Open Court.

Grant, Judith, and Peta Tancred. 1992. 'A feminist perspective on state bureaucracy', pp. 112–28 in *Gendering Organizational Analysis*, edited by A. J. Mills and P. Tancred. Newbury Park, Calif.: Sage.

Greenberg, David F. 1988. *The Construction of Homosexuality.* Chicago: University of Chicago Press.

Grosz, Elizabeth. 1994. *Volatile Bodies: Towards a Corporeal Feminism.* Sydney: Allen & Unwin.

Gutmann, Matthew C. 2001. 'Men and masculinities in Latin America', *Men and Masculinities* 3 (3), special issue.

Habermas, Jürgen. 1976. *Legitimation Crisis.* London: Heinemann.

Hacker, Helen Mayer. 1957. 'The new burdens of masculinity', *Marriage and Family Living* 19: 227–33.

Halpern, Diane F., and Mary L. LaMay. 2000. 'The smarter sex: a critical review of sex differences in intelligence', *Educational Psychology Review* 12: 229–46.

Harding, Sandra. 1986. *The Science Question in Feminism.* Ithaca, NY: Cornell University Press.

Herdt, Gilbert H. 1981. *Guardians of the Flutes: Idioms of Masculinity.* New York: McGraw-Hill.

Hochschild, Arlie Russell. 1983. *The Managed Heart: Commercialization of Human Feeling.* Berkeley: University of California Press.

Hocquenghem, Guy. 1978 [1972]. *Homosexual Desire*, translated by D. Dangoor. London: Allison & Busby.

Hogrebe, Mark C., Sherrie L. Nist and Isadore Newman. 1985. 'Are there gender differences in reading achievement? an investigation using the High School and Beyond data', *Journal of Educational Psychology* 77: 716–24.

Holland, Dorothy C., and Margaret A. Eisenhart. 1990. *Educated in Romance: Woman, Achievement, and College Culture.* Chicago: University of Chicago Press.

Hollway, Wendy. 1994. 'Separation, integration and difference: contradictions in a gender regime', pp. 247–69 in *Power/Gender*, edited by H. L. Radtke and J. S. Henderikus. London: Sage.

Holter, Øystein Gullvåg. 1995. 'Family theory reconsidered', pp. 99–129 in *Labour of Love: Beyond the Self-Evidence of Everyday Life*, edited by T. Borchgrevink and Ø. G. Holter. Aldershot: Avebury.

——1997. *Gender, Patriarchy and Capitalism: A Social Forms Analysis.* Oslo: University of Oslo.

hooks, bell. 1984. *Feminist Theory: From Margin to Center.* Boston: South End Press.

Hyde, Janet Shibley. 1984. 'How large are gender-differences in aggression? a developmental meta-analysis', *Developmental Psychology* 20: 722–36.

Hyde, Janet Shibley, and Nita M. McKinley. 1997. 'Gender differences in cognition: results from meta-analyses', pp. 30–51 in *Gender Differences in Human Cognition*, edited by P. J. Caplan, M. Crawford, J. S. Hyde and J. T. E. Richardson. New York: Oxford University Press.

Inter-Parliamentary Union. 1999. 'Women in national parliaments: situation as of 5 December', www.ipu.org/wmn-e/world/htm.

Irigaray, Luce. 1985 [1977]. *This Sex Which is Not One*, translated by C. Porter and C. Burke. Ithaca, NY: Cornell University Press.

Jackson, Peter A. 1997. '*Kathoey*><Gay><Man: The historical emergence of gay male identity in Thailand', pp. 166–90 in *Sites of Desire, Economies of Pleasure*, edited by L. Manderson and M. Jolley. Chicago: University of Chicago Press.

Jaffee, Sara, and Janet Shibley Hyde. 2000. 'Gender differences in moral orientation: a meta-analysis', *Psychological Bulletin* 126: 703–26.

Jeffords, Susan. 1989. *The Remasculinization of America: Gender and the Vietnam War.* Bloomington: Indiana University Press.

Kanter, Rosabeth. 1977. *Men and Women of the Corporation.* New York: Basic Books.

Kemper, Theodore D. 1990. *Social Structure and Testosterone: Explorations of the Socio-bio-social Chain.* New Brunswick: Rutgers University Press.

Kessler, Suzanne J., and Wendy McKenna. 1978. *Gender: An Ethnomethodological Approach.* New York: Wiley.

Kidd, Benjamin. 1898. *Social Evolution*, 3rd edition. London: Macmillan.

Kirk, David. 1993. *The Body, Schooling and Culture.* Geelong: Deakin University Press.

Klein, Alan M. 1993. *Little Big Men: Bodybuilding Subculture and Gender Construction.* Albany, NY: State University of New York Press.

Klein, Viola. 1946. *The Feminine Character: History of an Ideology.* London: Kegan Paul, Trench, Trubner & Co.

Kling, Kristen, Janet Shibley Hyde, Caroline J. Showers, and Brenda N. Buswell. 1999. 'Gender differences in self-esteem: a meta-analysis', *Psychological Bulletin* 125: 470–500.

Kollontai, Alexandra. 1977. *Selected Writings*, translated by A. Holt. London: Allison & Busby.

Komarovsky, Mirra. 1946. 'Cultural contradictions and sex roles', *American Journal of Sociology* 52: 184–9.

——1964. *Blue Collar Marriage.* New York: Vintage.

Krafft-Ebing, Richard von. 1965 [1886]. *Psychopathia Sexualis*, 12th edition. New York: Paperback Library.

Kristeva, Julia. 1984 [1974]. *Revolution in Poetic Language*. New York: Columbia University Press.

Laing, R. D. 1968. *The Politics of Experience*. New York: Ballantine Books.

Laplanche, J., and J.-B. Pontalis. 1973. *The Language of Psycho-Analysis*. New York: Norton.

Laqueur, Thomas Walter. 1990. *Making Sex: Body and Gender from the Greeks to Freud*. Cambridge, Mass.: Harvard University Press.

Laslett, Barbara, and Barrie Thorne, eds. 1997. *Feminist Sociology: Life Histories of a Movement*. New Brunswick: Rutgers University Press.

Laumann, Edward O., John H. Gagnon, Robert T. Michael and Stuart Michaels. 1994. *The Social Organization of Sexuality: Sexual Practices in the United States*. Chicago: University of Chicago Press.

Lee, Vicky, ed. 1999. *The Tranny Guide*, 7th edition. London: Way Out Publishing.

Lees, Sue. 1986. *Losing Out: Sexuality and Adolescent Girls*. London: Hutchinson.

Lenz, Ilse, Anja Szypulski, and Beate Molsich, eds. 1996. *Frauenbewegungen International: Eine Arbeitsbibliographie*. Opladen: Leske & Budrich.

Lessing, Doris. 1962. *The Golden Notebook*. London: Michael Joseph.

Lorber, Judith. 1994. *Paradoxes of Gender*. New Haven: Yale University Press.

Mac an Ghaill, Máirtín. 1994. *The Making of Men: Masculinities, Sexualities and Schooling*. Buckingham: Open University Press.

Maccoby, Eleanor E., ed. 1966. *The Development of Sex Differences*. Stanford, Calif.: Stanford University Press.

Maccoby, Eleanor E., and Carol Nagy Jacklin. 1975. *The Psychology of Sex Differences*. Stanford, Calif.: Stanford University Press.

MacKinnon, Catharine A. 1983. 'Feminism, marxism, method and the state: toward feminist jurisprudence', *Signs* 8: 635–58.

——1989. *Toward a Feminist Theory of the State*. Cambridge, Mass.: Harvard University Press.

Malinowski, Bronisław. 1927. *Sex and Repression in Savage Society*. London: Routledge & Kegan Paul.

Malos, Ellen, ed. 1980. *The Politics of Housework*. London: Allison & Busby.

Marchand, Marianne H., and Anne Sisson Runyan, eds. 2000. *Gender and Global Restructuring: Sightings, Sites and Resistances*. London: Routledge.

Marcuse, Herbert. 1955. *Eros and Civilization: A Philosophical Enquiry into Freud*. Boston: Beacon Press.

Marks, Elaine, and Isabelle de Courtivron, eds. 1981. *New French Feminisms: An Anthology*. Brighton: Harvester.

Mead, Margaret. 1963 [1935]. *Sex and Temperament in Three Primitive Societies*. New York: William Morrow.

Melville, Herman. 1969 [1853]. 'Bartleby the Scrivener', pp. 159–90 in *Alienation: A Casebook*, edited by D. J. Burrows and F. R. Lapides. New York: Crowell.

Menzies, Jackie, ed. 1998. *Modern Boy Modern Girl: Modernity in Japanese Art 1910–1935*. Sydney: Art Gallery of NSW.

Messerschmidt, James W. 1993. *Masculinities and Crime: Critique and Reconceptualization of Theory*. Lanham, Md.: Rowman & Littlefield.

——1997. *Crime as Structured Action: Gender, Race, Class and Crime in the Making*. Thousand Oaks, Calif.: Sage.

Messner, Michael A. 1997. *The Politics of Masculinities: Men in Movements*. Thousand Oaks, Calif.: Sage.

Mies, Maria. 1986. *Patriarchy and Accumulation on a World Scale: Women in the International Division of Labour*. London: Zed Books.

Mill, John Stuart. 1912 [1869]. *The Subjection of Women*, in *J. S. Mill: Three Essays*. London: Oxford University Press.

Millett, Kate. 1972. *Sexual Politics*. London: Abacus.

Mills, Albert J., and Peta Tancred, eds. 1992. *Gendering Organizational Analysis*. Newbury Park, Calif.: Sage.

Mitchell, Juliet. 1966. 'Women: the longest revolution', *New Left Review* 40: 11–37.

——1971. *Woman's Estate*. Harmondsworth: Penguin.

——1974. *Psychoanalysis and Feminism*. New York: Pantheon Books.

Mohanty, Chandra Talpade. 1991. 'Under Western eyes: feminist scholarship and colonial discourses', pp. 51–80 in *Third World Women and the Politics of Feminism*, edited by C. T. Mohanty, A. Russo and L. Torres. Bloomington: Indiana University Press.

Moodie, T. Dunbar, with Vivienne Ndatshe. 1994. *Going for Gold: Men, Mines and Migration*. Johannesburg: Witwatersrand University Press.

Morgan, Robin, ed. 1970. *Sisterhood is Powerful: An Anthology of Writings from the Women's Liberation Movement*. New York: Vintage.

Morgan, Sally. 1987. *My Place*. Fremantle: Fremantle Arts Centre Press.

Morrell, Robert, ed. 2001. *Changing Men in Southern Africa*. London: Zed Books.

Murray, Alison J. 1991. *No Money, No Honey: A Study of Street Traders and Prostitutes in Jakarta*. Singapore: Oxford University Press.

Nagel, Joane. 1998. 'Masculinity and nationalism: gender and sexuality in the making of nations', *Ethnic and Racial Studies* 21: 242–69.

Namaste, Viviane K. 2000. *Invisible Lives: The Erasure of Transsexual and Transgendered People*. Chicago: University of Chicago Press.

Naples, Nancy A., ed. 1998. *Community Activism and Feminist Politics: Organizing across Race, Class and Gender.* New York: Routledge.

Neale, J. E. 1960. *Queen Elizabeth I.* Harmondsworth: Penguin.

Nilsson, Arne. 1998. 'Creating their own private and public: the male homosexual life space in a Nordic city during high modernity', *Journal of Homosexuality* 35: 81–116.

Novikova, Irina. 2000. 'Soviet and post-Soviet masculinities: after men's wars in women's memories', pp. 117–29 in *Male Roles, Masculinities and Violence: A Culture of Peace Perspective*, edited by I. Breines, R. Connell and I. Eide. Paris: UNESCO Publishing.

O'Connor, Julia S., Ann Shola Orloff and Sheila Shaver. 1999. *States, Markets, Families: Gender, Liberalism and Social Policy in Australia, Canada, Great Britain and the United States.* Cambridge: Cambridge University Press.

O'Donnell, Mike, and Sue Sharpe. 2000. *Uncertain Masculinities: Youth, Ethnicity and Class in Contemporary Britain.* London: Routledge.

Oetomo, Dede. 1996. 'Gender and sexual orientation in Indonesia', pp. 259–69 in *Fantasizing the Feminine in Indonesia*, edited by L. J. Sears. Durham, NC: Duke University Press.

Pahl, J. M., and R. E. Pahl. 1972. *Managers and their Wives: A Study of Career and Family Relationships in the Middle Class.* Harmondsworth: Penguin.

Parker, Richard G. 1991. *Bodies, Pleasures and Passions: Sexual Culture in Contemporary Brazil.* Boston: Beacon Press.

Parsons, Talcott, and Robert F. Bales. 1956. *Family Socialization and Interaction Process.* London: Routledge & Kegan Paul.

Pateman, Carole. 1988. *The Sexual Contract.* Stanford, Calif.: Stanford University Press.

Perkins, Roberta. 1983. *The 'Drag Queen' Scene: Transsexuals in Kings Cross.* Sydney: Allen & Unwin.

Pleck, J. H., and J. Sawyer, eds. 1974. *Men and Masculinity.* Englewood Cliffs, NJ: Prentice-Hall.

Pollert, Anna. 1981. *Girls, Wives, Factory Lives.* London: Macmillan.

Pringle, Rosemary. 1989. *Secretaries Talk: Sexuality, Power and Work.* Sydney: Allen & Unwin.

——1992. 'Absolute sex? unpacking the sexuality/gender relationship', pp. 76–101 in *Rethinking Sex: Social Theory and Sexuality Research*, edited by R. W. Connell and G. W. Dowsett. Melbourne: Melbourne University Press.

Ram, Kalpana. 1991. *Mukkuvar Women: Gender, Hegemony and Capitalist Transformation in a South Indian Fishing Community.* Sydney: Allen & Unwin.

Reiter, Rayna Rapp. 1977. 'The search for origins: unravelling the threads of gender hierarchy', *Critique of Anthropology* 9 & 10: 5–24.

Risman, Barbara J. 1986. 'Can men "mother"? life as a single father', *Family Relations* 35: 95–102.

——1998. *Gender Vertigo: American Families in Transition*. New Haven: Yale University Press.

Roberts, Celia. 2000. 'Biological behaviour? hormones, psychology and sex', *NWSA Journal* 12: 1–20.

Rogers, Lesley. 2000. *Sexing the Brain*. London: Phoenix.

Roper, Michael. 1994. *Masculinity and the British Organization Man since 1945*. Oxford: Oxford University Press.

Rosenberg, Rosalind. 1982. *Beyond Separate Spheres: Intellectual Roots of Modern Feminism*. New Haven: Yale University Press.

Rowbotham, Sheila. 1969. *Women's Liberation and the New Politics*. Nottingham: Spokesman.

Rubin, Gayle. 1975. 'The traffic in women: notes on the "political economy" of sex', pp. 157–210 in *Toward an Anthropology of Woman*, edited by R. R. Reiter. New York: Monthly Review.

——1984. 'Thinking sex: notes for a radical theory of the politics of sexuality', pp. 267–319 in *Pleasure and Danger: Exploring Female Sexuality*, edited by C. S. Vance. Melbourne: Routledge & Kegan Paul.

——1991. 'The catacombs: a temple of the butthole', pp. 119–41 in *Leatherfolk: Radical Sex, People, Politics and Practice*, edited by M. Thompson. Boston: Alyson Publications.

Sahlins, Marshall. 1977. *The Use and Abuse of Biology: An Anthropological Critique of Sociobiology*. London: Tavistock.

Sartre, Jean-Paul. 1968. *Search for a Method*. Translated by H. Barnes. New York: Vintage.

Sawyer, Jack. 1974 [1970]. 'On male liberation', pp. 170–3 in *Men and Masculinity*, edited by J. H. Peck and J. Sawyer. Englewood Cliffs, NJ: Prentice-Hall.

Schofield, T., R. W. Connell, L. Walker, J. Wood and D. Butland. 2000. 'Understanding men's health: a gender relations approach to masculinity, health and illness', *Journal of American College Health* 48: 247–56.

Schools Commission (Australia). 1975. *Girls, School and Society*. Canberra: Schools Commission.

Schreiner, Olive. 1978 [1911]. *Woman and Labour*. London: Virago.

Scutt, Jocelynne A. 1985. *Growing Up Feminist: The New Generation of Australian Women*. Sydney: Angus & Robertson.

Segal, Lynne. 1994. *Straight Sex: Rethinking the Politics of Pleasure*. Berkeley: University of California Press.

Seifert, Ruth. 1993. *Individualisierungsprozesse, Geschlechterverhältnisse und die soziale Konstruktion des Soldaten*. Munich: Sozialwissenschaftliches Institut der Bundeswehr.

Semaw, S. 2000. 'The world's oldest stone artefacts from Gona, Ethiopia: their implications for understanding stone technology and patterns of human evolution between 2.6–1.5 million years ago', *Journal of Archaeological Science* 27: 1197–1214.

Severiens, Sabine, and Geer ten Dam. 1998. 'A multi-level analysis of gender differences in learning orientations', *British Journal of Educational Psychology* 68: 595–608.

Slapšak, Svetlana. 2000. 'Hunting, ruling, sacrificing: tradional male practices in contemporary Balkan culture', pp. 131–42 in *Male Roles, Masculinities and Violence: A Culture of Peace Perspective*, edited by I. Breines, R. W. Connell and I. Eide. Paris: UNESCO Publishing.

Smith, Dorothy. 1987. *The Everyday World as Problematic: A Feminist Sociology*. Toronto: University of Toronto Press.

——1990. *The Conceptual Practices of Power: A Feminist Sociology of Knowledge*. Boston: Northeastern University Press.

Smith, T. W., and R. J. Smith. 1994. 'Changes in firearm ownership among women, 1980–1994'. Paper presented to conference of American Society of Criminology, Miami.

Stacey, Judith. 1983. *Patriarchy and Socialist Revolution in China*. Berkeley: University of California Press.

Staudt, Kathleen, ed. 1997. *Women, International Development and Politics: The Bureaucratic Mire*. Philadelphia: Temple University Press.

Steele, Valerie. 1996. *Fetish: Fashion, Sex and Power*. New York: Oxford University Press.

Stienstra, Deborah. 2000. 'Dancing resistance from Rio to Beijing: transnational women's organizing and United Nations conferences, 1992–6', pp. 209–24 in *Gender and Global Restructuring*, edited by M. H. Marchand and A. S. Runyan. London: Routledge.

Stoller, Robert J. 1968. *Sex and Gender*, vol. 1: *On the Development of Masculinity and Femininity*. London: Hogarth Press.

Stopes, Marie. 1933 [1918]. *Married Love*, 21st edition. London: Putnam.

Strathern, Marilyn. 1978. 'The achievement of sex: paradoxes in Hagen gender-thinking', pp. 171–202 in *The Yearbook of Symbolic Anthropology*, edited by E. Schwimmer. London: Hurst.

Tanaka, Kazuko. 1977. *A Short History of the Women's Movement in Modern Japan*, 3rd edition. Japan: Femintern Press.

Tannen, Deborah. 1990. *You Just Don't Understand: Women and Men in Conversation*. New York: Morrow.

Theberge, Nancy. 1991. 'Reflections on the body in the sociology of sport', *Quest* 43: 123–34.

Thorne, Barrie. 1993. *Gender Play: Girls and Boys in School.* New Brunswick: Rutgers University Press.

Thorne, Barrie, Marjorie Faulstich Orellana, Wan Shun Eva Lam and Anna Chee. Forthcoming. 'Raising children, and growing up, across national borders: comparative perspectives on age, gender, and migration', in *Gender and U.S. Immigration*, edited by Pierrette Hondagneu-Sotelo. Berkeley: University of California Press.

Tohidi, Nayereh. 1991. 'Gender and Islamic fundamentalism: feminist politics in Iran', pp. 251–65 in *Third World Women and the Politics of Feminism*, edited by C. T. Mohanty, A. Russo and L. Torres. Bloomington: Indiana University Press.

Tomsen, Stephen. 1998. '"He had to be a poofter or something": violence, male honour and heterosexual panic', *Journal of Interdisciplinary Gender Studies* 3(2): 44–57.

Torres, Lourdes. 1991. 'The construction of the self in U.S. Latina biographies', pp. 271–87 in *Third World Women and the Politics of Feminism*, edited by C. T. Mohanty, A. Russo and L. Torres. Bloomington: Indiana University Press.

Troiden, Richard R. 1989. 'The formation of homosexual identities', *Journal of Homosexuality* 17: 43–73.

Turner, Bryan S. 1984. *The Body and Society.* Oxford: Basil Blackwell.

Twenge, Jean M. 1997. 'Changes in masculine and feminine traits over time: a meta-analysis', *Sex Roles* 36: 305–25.

United Nations Development Programme. 1999. *Human Development Report.* New York: Oxford University Press.

Vaerting, Mathilde [writing as Mathilde and Mathias Vaerting]. 1981 [1921]. *The Dominant Sex: A Study in the Sociology of Sex Differentiation.* Westport, Conn.: Hyperion.

Valdés, Teresa, and Enrique Gomáriz. 1995. *Latin American Women: Compared Figures.* Santiago: Instituto de la Mujer and FLACSO.

Vance, Carole. 1989. 'Social construction theory: problems in the history of sexuality', pp. 13–34 in *Homosexuality, Which Homosexuality?* edited by D. Altman et al. Amsterdam: Uitgeverij An Dekker/Schorer.

Vickers, Jill. 1994. 'Notes toward a political theory of sex and power', pp. 174–93 in *Power/Gender*, edited by H. L. Radtke and J. S. Henderikus. London: Sage.

Waetjen, Thembisa, and Gerhard Maré. 2001. '"Men amongst men": masculinity and Zulu nationalism in the 1980s', pp. 195–206 in *Changing Men in Southern Africa*, edited by R. Morrell. London: Zed Books.

Wajcman, Judy. 1999. *Managing like a Man: Women and Men in Corporate Management.* Cambridge: Polity and Sydney: Allen & Unwin.

Walby, Sylvia. 1990. *Theorizing Patriarchy.* Oxford: Basil Blackwell.

Wall, Diana di Zerega. 1994. *The Archaeology of Gender: Separating the Spheres in Urban America*. New York: Plenum Press.

Ward, Lester F. 1897 [1883]. *Dynamic Sociology, or Applied Social Science*, 2nd edition. New York: Appleton.

Weedon, Chris. 1987. *Feminist Practice and Poststructuralist Theory*. Oxford: Basil Blackwell.

Weeks, Jeffrey. 1977. *Coming Out: Homosexual Politics in Britain, from the Nineteenth Century to the Present*. London: Quartet.

——1986. *Sexuality*. London: Horwood & Tavistock.

Weitz, Rose, ed. 1998. *The Politics of Women's Bodies: Sexuality, Appearance and Behavior*. New York: Oxford University Press.

West, Candace, and Don H. Zimmerman. 1987. 'Doing gender', *Gender and Society* 1: 125–51.

Wexler, Philip. 1992. *Becoming Somebody: Toward a Social Psychology of School*. London: Falmer.

White, Patrick. 1979. *The Twyborn Affair*. London: Cape.

Wilson, Elizabeth. 1987. *Adorned in Dreams: Fashion and Modernity*. Berkeley: University of California Press.

Wollstonecraft, Mary. 1975 [1792]. *Vindication of the Rights of Woman*. Harmondsworth: Penguin.

Yeatman, Anna. 1990. *Bureaucrats, Technocrats, Femocrats: Essays on the Contemporary Australian State*. Sydney: Allen & Unwin.

Yuval-Davis, Nira. 1997. *Gender and Nation*. London: Sage.

Zulehner, Paul M., and Rainer Volz. 1998. *Männer im Aufbruch: Wie Deutschlands Männer sich selbst und wie Frauen sie sehen*. Ostfildern: Schwabenverlag.

Index of Names

Index of Topics